HOW I GOT CULTURED

Phyllis Barber

How I

Got Cultured

A NEVADA MEMOIR

University of Nevada Press
Reno   Las Vegas   London

How I Got Cultured: A Nevada Memoir was first published by the
University of Georgia Press in 1992. The 1994 University of
Nevada Press edition reproduces the original except for the
front matter, which has been modified to reflect the new publisher.

University of Nevada Press, Reno, Nevada 89557 USA
www.unpress.nevada.edu
Manufactured in the United States of America

Library of Congress Cataloging-in-Publication Data
Barber, Phyllis, 1943–
How I got culture: a Nevada memoir / Phyllis Barber.
p. cm.
Originally published: Athens: University of Georgia, c1992
ISBN 978-0-87417-233-1 (paperback : alk. paper)
1. Barber, Phyllis, 1943– —Childhood and youth. 2. Nevada—
Biography. 3. Mormons—Nevada—Biography. I. Title.
CT275.B3675A3 1994
979.3'033'092—dc20
[B]   93-38160
                                                               CIP

The paper used in this book is a recycled stock made from 30 percent
post-consumer waste materials, certified by FSC, and meets the require-
ments of American National Standard for Information Sciences—
Permanence of Paper for Printed Library Materials, ANSI/NISO Z39.48-1992
(R2002). Binding materials were selected for strength and durability.

This book has been reproduced as a digital reprint.

Winner of the Associated Writing Programs
Award for Creative Nonfiction

What he imagines
is so much more powerful
than facts.

David Malouf,
An Imaginary Life

To the real Nevada,
the Las Vegas High School Class of '61,
and the Rhythmettes—may they kick forever

CONTENTS

Portions of this memoir originally appeared, in slightly different form, in the following publications:

"Oh, Say Can You See?" in *Utah Holiday*
"Bird of Paradise" in *Dialogue: A Journal of Mormon Thought*
"At the Talent Show" in *The Missouri Review*

I am grateful to many people who have shown an interest in this project and wish to mention a few whose comments and encouragement have been especially helpful: Paul Swenson, Carol Houck Smith, François Camoin, Joe David Bellamy, and, as always, David Barber.

HOW I GOT CULTURED

INTRODUCTION

*T*wo dark-blue squad cars stopped too suddenly, one in front of me, one in back. I was only crossing the street. "Stop right there," the driver in the car behind me said sharply, each word distinct.

I hugged my pillow and teddy bear and shivered in my brown scuffed shoes in the first sun of early morning in Boulder City, Nevada. Four government rangers, two in each car, were staring at me as I twisted my head from back to front. They were interrupting my slow shuffle toward home after a slumber party, stopping me while everyone else in town was still asleep.

"The bulletin says she's eight and has dark hair." The same driver who told me to stop pulled his ratchety emergency brake and leaned out the window. "What's your name, little girl?" He wore an olive drab ranger hat and frightening sunglasses.

"I'm me," I said, barely able to move my tongue.

"What's your father's name?" the same man asked.

"Herman Nelson," I said into my bear's forehead.

"Speak up, would you?" the officer prodded.

"Herman Nelson," I said only slightly louder.

"What does he do for a living?"

"Sells insurance."

They held a conference. Then the driver leaned out again, his mirrored sunglasses reflecting me back to myself—small, skinny, black hair mussed from last night's pillow fights, eyes and the skin beneath them dark shadows from so little sleep. I felt wispy between the two squad cars with official insignias—the seal of the U.S. government, the words "Boulder City Rangers" painted inside a white sawtooth circle. The cars felt like Hoover Dam. I was the river; they were the dam. Big men. Big cars stopping me on my way home.

"Ranger Johnson here says he might know your dad," the driver said. "He's not sure, but he's not unsure either." His laugh was more like a snort. "So what else can you tell us?"

"My dad is the bishop." My voice quivered.

"The bishop of what?" the driver asked, snorting again. "Have we got a little Roman Catholic illegitimate here?"

"The Mormon bishop," I said, swallowing what little saliva was left in my mouth. I knew some people didn't like Mormons. My parents told us not to advertise.

"Those people with all the wives?" he asked as he rested his head on his arm and hung over the window frame.

"They don't do that anymore," Ranger Johnson said, leaning forward in the front seat and peering over the driver's shoulder.

"Why not?" the driver asked. "Sounds like a good deal to me. Different girl every night."

"She's probably who she says she is." Ranger Johnson settled back into his side of the car. "I think I've heard of her dad."

"Sure about that?"

"Let her go."

"You sure?"

"C'mon. We have other things to do."

"The little fish that got away," the driver said in a way that made me know I didn't like him or never would. "But don't you be running away, now, will you, little girl?" He waved, a big, slow hand, somehow smug with the certainty of his badge and his hat and his big blue car. Both squad cars crunched gravel and slowly rolled away, leaving me standing alone, near freezing on that warm, sunny morning.

I lived in Boulder City until I was twelve, before my family moved twenty-five miles away to another planet called Las Vegas. Boulder City was built in the early 1930s as the base of operation for the construction of Hoover Dam. It was a federal reservation, not unlike an Indian reservation, and was governed by federal appointees. State law had no say. It was a clean town. It was a dry town, even after Prohibition was repealed. It was an anomaly in the state of Nevada.

Built from a master plan, unlike other Nevada settlements, Boulder City was well tended and Midwest-like. It boasted trees and parks planted by a government horticulturist whose real name was Wilbur Weed. The major streets were Colorado, Wyoming, Arizona, Nevada, California, Utah, and New Mexico—the seven Colorado River Basin states—though when I skipped over them on my way to Boulder City Elementary, it never occurred to me their names had a purpose.

To me, they were wide rivers of black asphalt carrying people in cars, sizzling the bottoms of bare feet in the summertime, and hosting a parade every Fourth of July—Veterans of Foreign Wars, flag after flag after flag, marching bands from Clark County high schools, an open car filled with Miss Boulder City and her attendants, "America" being played over the public announcement system, drums beating out the rhythm of the United States of America.

The U.S. Government was everywhere—rows of brick houses built for government employees; flags flying on poles; the rangers; several veterans in the neighborhood, notably Mr. Goetz who kept a German shepherd attack dog from World War II enclosed be-

hind a twelve-foot fence in his backyard; and the Bureau of Recla-
mation's administration building at the top of the slanted terrain
of the city.

Whenever I was anywhere near this building, I had the feeling of not wanting to go any nearer. I don't even remember a
door being there. It seemed an impregnable fortress to me, even
though its expansive lawns provided grass for picnics and a cool
place to sit in the heat. The building was always visible from my
school's playground and in my peripheral vision. It was a constant
reminder of the miracles of engineering and evidence of man's
technological skill but also, it seemed to me, a constant sentinel
posted to watch over the town.

The city was divided in subtle ways: official and unofficial. During the dam's construction, trim brick houses had been built near
the administration building for government engineers and geolo-
gists. But for the ordinary workers of the Six Companies Construction Company, temporary wooden houses had been thrown
up in a day and a half at the bottom of the hill. These frame
houses were meant to be temporary, but my father, who needed
any home for his growing family, bought one for $400 after the
dam was completed.

I was aware of the differences between the high and low end of
town just as I was constantly aware of the dam, only a few miles
away, which channeled the Colorado River into diversion tunnels
and hummed steadily as it manufactured electricity and sent it
across the desert to California on high wires and transformers.

"We wouldn't be here without that dam," my father's brother,
Uncle Tommy, often said when he came over to help with household repairs. "Think of southern California," my father would say.
"Place'd go dark in a second without the dam." "And," Tommy
would add, "it keeps that unruly Colorado from wrecking people's
property."

The Hoover Dam's gigantic concrete face, its high overhead

cables that stretched across the canyon and swayed when the wind blew, its giant skeleton transformers that spanned the desert like long-legged spiders, and the artificial blue of Lake Mead where dusty brown canyons should have been put a nameless fear in me. I'd been taught that being a good Mormon was the most important thing anyone could ever think of doing and that everything on earth was only transient, sandwiched between the preexistence and the hereafter. I'd been told to keep my sights set on eternity—the world beyond this veil of tears. My life was but a small part of the eternal scheme, a miniscule speck in the overall plan of existence, except that God loved me.

This dam, which magnetized hundreds of thousands of visitors to its site every year, conflicted with my young sense of order. It was temporal, yet huge, solid, and certain of its place on the river. But human beings who trusted in the arm of flesh were not supposed to be wise. When Uncle Tommy talked about the dam lasting forever, I knew he didn't know much.

Everything man-made had feet of clay, as in King Nebuchadnezzar's dream in the Book of Daniel. Gold, silver, brass, and iron. Nothing would last except God. The dam would break into pieces someday; wind and water would carry the pieces away and roar through the canyons again with no regard for anything humans had built.

While everything was neat, tidy, and ordered in Boulder City and at the dam, the Mormon church had neat and tidy answers for everyone's salvation. The city was proud of its gift to the seven engineering wonders of the world; the Mormons were proud to be members of the only true church, the only church with the answers to the questions of "Who am I? Where did I come from? Where am I going?" But something about the certainty of both positions bothered my need for mystery, even as I enjoyed the benefits from both.

"If you make the gospel your first priority," speakers instructed us in Sacrament Meeting, "you will be rewarded with true happiness." My mother echoed the sentiment at the dinner table and while drying dishes. She wanted the church thick in our blood, and my father backed her 100 percent. "We believe with every fiber of our being," they told us often.

Except for Red Cross swimming lessons at Lake Mead in the summer, trips to ride the elevator down into the dam's insides, the public library, Ham's Grocery Store, piano lessons, school, or walking or roller-skating up and down the alphabet streets A, B, C, D, E through M, we were always at church: Sunday School, Sacrament Meeting, Relief Society for the women, MIA or Mutual Improvement Association for the teenagers, Primary for the children.

Except once, when my sister Elaine's joints and heart muscles were inflamed with rheumatic fever, and we were quarantined for two weeks. None of us could go to church, the first time most of us had ever missed a meeting. I felt sequestered, cloistered, and holy while we knelt around my sister's bed to pray to God for Elaine. My father anointed her forehead with consecrated olive oil, laid his hands on her head, and gave her a blessing in the name of the priesthood he'd been given by the church. Afterward, we all squeezed hands in the hope of bringing her back to health even if the requisite number of two priesthood holders weren't present for the blessing.

And yet, in between meals, chores, and our ministerings, I sat next to the picture window, my chin resting on my folded arms, and watched people on the street as if they were a movie and I were a stealthy jungle dweller behind vines and wet leaves: a soldier in the bushes who didn't march with any battalion. I'd recently seen a World War II film set on a tropical island.

I was quietly happy with those two weeks of independence during which I could drift free from the responsibilities of church and school, a little pod whirling off on its own to land somewhere and grow into something new and apart. A little pod that didn't know the way, that could blow where it would and listen to what it wanted. But then Elaine revived, and it was back to church and to the people who gave speeches and bore testimonies as to the truthfulness of the gospel. They were absolutely sure they were witnesses for God.

We did have good times at church—singing songs, learning to cross-stitch samplers that instructed us to "Greet the day with a song," playing Red Rover with our friends after meetings, and watching movies in Primary one summer when our leaders decided to give us a break from the Bible and Book of Mormon stories we'd heard so many times. When they turned off the lights and turned on a flickering projector every Wednesday morning, we watched a panorama of people from Nigeria, Egypt, Switzerland, Brazil, Russia, and China. They were ordinary people working, planting cotton, herding cows, even some bare-breasted African women carrying baskets of melons on their heads. We watched them sing and dance; we heard about their major crops and annual rainfall.

"Someday," the Primary president said, "I can bear witness to you, these people will accept the gospel of Jesus Christ of Latter-day Saints. And then the world will be a better place in which to live. Some of you will be missionaries who convert them."

I tried to imagine myself a missionary, but sometimes at night, I thought very quiet thoughts only I could hear. What if everyone were a Mormon and followed the same path to God? Wouldn't the world be too much the same? Everybody speaking the same language and thinking in the same way about God? Everybody saying family prayer in the morning and night, until every household had holes in the carpets from their boney knees? Then the women in Nigeria couldn't dance without blouses. Mr. Ripley next door couldn't drink beer every night and sing to the constellations, something I enjoyed as I lay by the open window searching with the palm of my hand for cold spots on my pillow.

But when my father was asked to be bishop of the Boulder City Ward, the spiritual leader of our local community of Mormons, I kept my private thoughts even from myself. I mustn't hide anything in my heart or in my mind now that our family was a vital part of the circle of faith, my father a leader for the saints. "All of you must set a good example for the others in the ward," my father told us, and that included me.

For a few years, I became a believer, no questions asked. I believed in my father, in his position, in his faith, in his authority in our household; I believed in our town, in its law and order, in its protected place in the bosom of the government's care; I even believed in the government's right to design a concrete structure to stop the flow of a mighty river and create order for the earth. I believed in everything because I needed to be unified with my family. After all, we were supposed to live together in the hereafter.

If I had to stop time, I'd stop it there where we were united in our certainty. Right there, at that spot, where my father was an important man, when our family and the ward members revered him and his new position. My father was happy; my family was sure of our place. I'd stop time right at that moment, before the test jets from Nellis Air Force Base began splitting the sky every day with a sonic boom, before the test sites and the atom bomb clouds that flowered on the early morning horizon, too big for me to comprehend.

But soon after that, the certainty to which I'd given myself began to warp and shift.

One of the members of the congregation, Brother Morgan, stuck a rifle in his mouth and pulled the trigger. My father walked to the dark apartment with a bucket and clean rags. He wouldn't talk about it, even when we asked, "Why? What happened? Tell us, Daddy."

Something happened then. My father had been not only the bishop of the Boulder City Ward, but a member of Rotary and the city council, too. He was handsome, charming, well liked in his hexagonal eyeglasses, comforting with his compassionate smile. But something happened—some turning of his self to a different angle, some shifting of ground. He seemed to veer off in a different direction, away from the responsibility of spiritual leadership for the Boulder City Ward, of having people call to discuss their problems or pull triggers to tell him the truth of their lives. It seemed as though he put his hands over his ears and drove fast into Las Vegas and found a small isolated house on the edge of the desert, unable to hide in the certainty anymore.

Our family was ejected from what had become a solid life in a solid government town. We landed on the edge of the desert where the wind tore up my mind while I slept. I landed in an alien elementary school where dust blew against the green-colored cinder block and sloped two feet high against the building.

Though we were at the desert's edge, I sometimes couldn't see it. The thin boundary shifted with the wind, barely discernible as the dust covered the asphalt road in front of our home and turned it into a sandy floor over and over again.

I waited for something to pull me back into certainty. Maybe God, whom I suspected lived in the center of the blazing sun omnipresent in the desert. He could pull me in, reel me toward the center of surety. But nothing pulled from anywhere, not the government, which didn't appear to be in this new place. Not my church.

My father had somehow dismantled the bricks of faith in my mind when he resigned from his position of bishop. No one was supposed to resign. Faithful servants stayed in that office until they were released. My father both resigned and fled.

Now his church position was to be in charge of a group of twelve-year-old boys in our new ward. In my mind, these boys were supposed to be respectful because they'd been newly or-

dained to the priesthood. But when we had a get-acquainted bar-
becue for them in our backyard, they pantsed each other and
laughed like crazies out of control.

This wasn't how things were before. And breasts weren't growing on my chest, even though my menstrual period had started.
I didn't know if I'd ever be a woman. Nothing seemed perfect
anymore.

I was thrown into uncertainty for the first time. It seemed as
though we were like Adam and Eve's family, expelled from the
Garden of Eden to wander in the wilderness. I wanted to recapture the green trees and the ever-blooming oleander bushes
in Boulder City's parks, the absolute certainty of government
jurisdiction and complete faith in religious promises. But when
I awoke in the middle of the night, I sensed those things were
behind me. I had to find a new life. The old one was gone.

In a sense, I'm still trying to find that life, having been de-
railed by the confusion of adolescence and later by the obligations
of adulthood, but I need clues from the past as I move on. What
was the milieu surrounding me as a child: the suppositions, the
beliefs, the attitudes? Who were those people: my relatives, the
rangers, the teachers in my church? And finally, need I always be
a product of southern Nevada and the Mormon church? Made in
the U.S.A. and Nevada by the Mormons? Am I a flower that can
bloom anywhere, or will my roots shrivel in strange soil?

OH, SAY
CAN YOU SEE?

*O*ver a radio microphone, into the nation's and FDR's ears, Grandma sang "The Star-Spangled Banner." "Oh, say can you see," she sang, my grandma who ironed for nickels and scrubbed for dimes, "by the dawn's early light, what so proudly we hailed?" Everybody in Boulder City recommended her for the program because they'd heard her at lots of funerals.

A big black open car full of VIPs delivered her home from the dedication ceremony. She waved good-bye. That's what my daddy told me.

I think she sang by the memorial, in between the statues— broad-chested men flanked by tall stiff wings pointing skyward. I hope those ninety-six men who died building the dam got fluffier wings, or else they probably never will fly out of their graves.

More than anything, I remember the dam and that story about Grandma. But there was an atom bomb test too—a rip in the sky, a gash that showed the sky's insides for a minute. I remember thinking about my Band-Aid box. I never could have unwrapped enough Band-Aids even if I had pulled the red string exactly down the side crease without tearing into the flat side of the paper where the red letters are printed. After that minute passed, the sky's blood and the earth's dust made a big cloud, a busy one. It drifts over my mind sometimes.

I got my first chance at swearing because of Hoover Dam—"I went to the dam to get some dam water. I asked the dam man for some of his dam water and the dam man said no."

Damns were frowned on at my house. So I chanted the forbidden whenever I could, with a flourish, making sure Mama and Daddy heard.

Actually, we called it Boulder Dam. At one time or another, everybody talked about jumping off or sliding down the curving concrete, but nobody did it except one time a man from New York did. His note said he lost his money gambling in Las Vegas and that nothing mattered anyway.

"He looked like a mass of jelly," said Uncle Tommy, an electrician at the dam.

"Could you see his face at all?" I asked.

"It was like a leaky puzzle, liquid in the cracks."

I wanted to ask more, but my Aunt Grace changed the subject.

Whenever anybody came to visit we always took them to see the dam. Down to Black Canyon, down to 120 degrees in the shade where heat ricocheted off sizzling boulders.

Every time, even now, I stop at the memorial on the Nevada side. The two bronzed angels stand guard over a message: "It is fitting that the flag of our country should fly in honor of those men . . . inspired by a vision of lonely lands made fruitful." My sister Elaine used to say that some of them fell off scaffolds into wet, pouring cement. Concrete soup. I always looked to see if a hand or a foot stuck out anywhere in the dam and checked for bumps on the surface.

The cloud had bumps, swollen and bulging. I've seen many shapes of clouds in my life—lambs, potatoes, even alligators, but I saw only one like that lumpy mushroom. Its cap reminded me of the North Wind, the puffy-cheeked one who bets with the Sun and blows fiercely to get coats off people's backs. Instead of sky and trees, it blew into the earth and got everything back in its face—sand, splintered tumbleweeds, thousands of years of rocks battering their own kind, crashing, colliding against each other, the dry desert silt, jaggedly rising from ribboned gullies and rain patterns on the sand, rising into a cloud that looked like a mushroom capped by the swollen-cheeked North Wind.

My father was proud of Hoover Dam. He helped build it, drove trucks hauling fill. He also loved the desert. Mama never thought much of it, not much at all.

"Herman, it's so hot here, so dusty. No creeks, no greenery. It's not human to live here."

My daddy always smiled when she started in. I liked his smile when she seemed unhappy.

"Herman, can't we move before it's too late?"

Daddy never argued this subject. He just reminded Mama of his mother, the grandma who sang, and how she saved her family with a letter to her relative: "Can't find work. We've tried everything in the Great Basin—farming in Idaho, mining in Nevada, selling shoes in Utah. Thought you might have a place for my husband and sons helping on that big new dam."

"It seemed like we were heading for Mecca, it did," he used to say. "All those mirages on the highway and our tires never getting wet. Sunshine, wide open-armed skies, and promises."

"Promises? Of what?" Mama asked. "How can you cultivate rocks in Black Canyon, Hoover Dam cement, the sand, the sage, the yucca?"

"I have a job, a wife, three children, and an address," he said. "God bless the government."

The one time Mama did leave the desert and the dam, the time when my father put on his navy uniform with the brass buttons to go sailing in the Pacific, she wasn't treated as she should have been. Daddy always reminded her. Mother thought her relatives would help out with me and Elaine when she moved to Idaho Falls, Idaho, but all extra hands were needed for milking, haying, harvesting potatoes.

"I'm sorry, but—" they all said.

Mama taught school—six grades in one room. She was tired at night when she picked me up from the scratch-and-bite nursery school for war orphans. She didn't talk much then, so I looked for Daddy under the covers, under the bed, and in the bathtub.

"Why did Daddy go away? Is he coming back?"

Mama read letters to us, words like China, Okinawa, kamikaze, Battleship *Missouri*, destroyers, phrases like "I miss you," "When the war is over," and "When we get back home to Boulder City, I'll roll down Administration Hill with Elaine and Phyllis."

Rolling. Me rolling, repeating my face to the green grass. The cloud rolling, repeating itself to the open sky. And deep inside the busy cloud topped by the North Wind puffing in the wrong direction, a fire burned. Not a bonfire, but a tall fire hedged by a column of jumbled whites, browns, and grays. A thick fire mostly hidden but not quite. Black smoke twisted away from the red fire, sometimes losing itself in the confusion, sometimes slithering out into the blue. The cloud burned, scarring its belly, melting its insides with red and yellow while it rolled over and over in the same place.

We still pass Administration Hill every time we drive to the dam to go on the world's longest elevator ride, dropping down deep into the stomach, the belly of Hoover, to the hum of big red generators with white round lights on top.

The guide always talks about kilowatts, power to southern California, and spillover precautions. I used to watch the ant tractors and drivers circling the generators stories below while he explained.

"Now if you'll follow me, we'll go directly into the Nevada

diversion tunnel," a voice from a bullhorn said. Our feet echoed through a dripping cave, man-blasted, the voice said.

Water roared through a giant gray penstock (the guide called it) under the square observation room. I barely heard his speech. He pointed to yellow, red, blue, and green lines on a painted chart under a green metal lampshade. Outside the glassed, chicken-wired window, a man balanced on a catwalk to check bolts twice his size. The room trembled. The water rushed. I was glad I didn't have to tightrope catwalks and check pipes as big as the world.

"If you'll step this way, I'll lead you now to the base of the dam. Watch your step, ladies and gentlemen."

Outside, we looked up, up, everywhere up. Big cables stretched across, miles overhead—cables that lowered tons of railroad cars onto the tracks where we stood. I moved my toe quickly at the thought. Over the edge of the wall, the Colorado whirled green pools into white foam.

One time I told my mother the river must be mad.

"Rivers don't get angry, Phyllis," she said.

"This one does. It doesn't like going through all those tunnels and generators. It would suck me down forever if I fell in."

"You won't fall in. Mother's here to protect you."

Reassured, I ran from the wall to the center point where I could spread-eagle across two states.

"Ma'am," blared the bullhorn, "will you kindly keep your child with the tour group?"

My mother jerked me back into Arizona, told me to stop wandering off, to stay with the group.

Once when I was about six, Uncle Tommy scooped me into his arms. The temperature must have been 128 degrees that day.

"See, Phyllis honey. See the steepest, longest slide on earth." He not only held me up, but leaned me over the edge to see better.

"Uncle Tommy. Put me down." I kicked and squirmed.

"Not yet, honey. Look at the big river down there. We stopped that river. We did it. Look. We harnessed it. That's where you were a few minutes ago on the tour. See the railroad tracks?" He held me with only one arm as he pointed.

"Uncle Tommy. Put me down. Please. I don't like to look there." My head buried into his gray uniform but got stopped at the metal numbers on his badge.

"Ah, come on honey. Uncle Tommy wouldn't let anything happen to you." He still held me so I could see over the edge.

"Let me down. Let me down."

"Gee, why are you so upset. I wouldn't—"

I ran away from his words, away to the car that boiled the closest two feet of air around its metal surface. The door handle was untouchable, unopenable. I couldn't hide away to cry. I had to do it in the air, on top of that dam, in front of people from Manila, Cheyenne, and Pittsburgh.

I used to wonder if there had been devils in that redfire cloud. My mother always talked about how devils like fire and red and gambling, even how the world would end by fire because of them. I imagined horns balancing on top of their red caps that buttoned tight, holding all that cunning close between their ears while they rolled and tumbled in the churning clouds, while the fire burned yellow and red at the center and in my eyes when I think about it.

One night after Uncle Tommy leaned me out over the edge of the dam, he and my mother balanced a bed on the overhead cables, thousands of feet above concrete and water.

"You have disobeyed again," Mama said. "Always running off."

"I'm sorry."

"You'll have to sleep out there tonight, Phyllis. Maybe you'll learn to listen."

"Please, Mother, not at the dam. I'll be good. I'll listen. I won't go away without telling you ever again."

"Just climb up the ladder, honey," said Uncle Tommy. "Nothing to worry about."

"Please no," I said as I climbed the ladder, up, up, high above the scenic viewpoint where tourists said "ooh" and "aahhh." The wind blew, the cables rose and fell and twirled jump rope. I wore my blue furry Donald Duck slippers and my rosy chenille bathrobe, and I put one and then another foot ahead, in front. For a minute I walked on the wind and wasn't afraid. Then I got to the creaking bed, leaning downside at every shift in weight.

"Rock-a-bye baby," Mama sang from the cliff's edge. "Hush-a-bye." Uncle Tommy accompanied her on his trumpet.

The bed started to slip. The bedsprings scraped over the cables, fingernails on a blackboard, slipping one by one.

"Mama," I screamed.

Mama leaned as far out over the edge as she could while Uncle Tommy held her knees. We stretched for each other. Like long, rubbery, airless balloons we stretched and stretched, arching, reaching, trying to connect.

"Hold me, Mama."

Our fingertips only pointed at each other as I passed.

I tried to make a sail out of the quilt. I stood up to catch the wind with it but couldn't keep my balance. One Donald Duck slipper, followed by the other, followed by me in rosy chenille, sailed through the night toward the dam to get some dam water from the dam man.

After it mushroomed, the cloud started to break apart and dot the sky, and I thought of the time I climbed a leafless tree. Instead of watching where I was going, I talked to Rocky, my dog, who jumped and yelped at the bottom. Someone else had broken the twig that raked my cheek, that beaded the slash with red. A necklace of red pearls, almost. Dot dash dot. A design that stared at me in the mirror until it got better and faded away just like the cloud did.

Everybody wants to see the dam. It's famous. One day when I was about ten, another big black car, open and full of important men, drove through Boulder City. Flags stuck out on both sides of the windshield, rippling. I tried every possible angle to see Ike, running around legs, pushing through to openings but finding none. I was missing everything. Everybody who had closed shop and home for the afternoon was crowding to see Ike, too.

"Daddy, hold me up so I can see."

His dark blue uniformed arms full of baby brother, he pointed to the sill of Central Market's picture window. Stacks of returnable glass bottles towered behind the pane and wiggled every time a reflected parade watcher moved.

I climbed to the ledge as the fire engine and two police cars sirened past. Even standing there, I could see only flashing red lights, the backs of heads, and an occasional helium balloon drifting, ownerless.

"Daddy, I can't see."

Somehow he managed to pick me up in time. Ike, his uniform dotted with brass and ribbons, looked just like the *Newsreel* pictures at the Boulder Theatre. He smiled and waved just like on *Newsreel*, too. I didn't need to see him after all. I already knew.

I liked the high school band best. The flags and the band.

"Children," my daddy said at the dinner table that night, "you are lucky to live in America." His blue eyes moistened as they always did when he talked about God and country. We all knelt by our chairs, and Daddy said, "We thank thee for such men as General Eisenhower to lead our great country. Bless our friends and relatives. Help us to live in peace. In the name of Jesus Christ, amen."

I saw Ike again on *Newsreel* several weeks later. He was still waving and smiling, framed by the granite-like building blocks of the dam. He didn't look too big next to the dam. Neither did his friends.

One morning, about five o'clock, our gray Plymouth drove in the opposite direction from the dam, toward Las Vegas, out by

Railroad Pass where Uncle Tommy played trumpet on Saturday night. Elaine and I kept warm under a friendship quilt and read the embroidered names of Mama's old friends, waiting.

"It's time," Daddy said. "Watch. Don't miss this. We should be able to see everything, even if it is seventy-five miles away."

We waited some more, eating apples and crackers.

"It's got to be time," he said.

My neck cramped. I looked at the sunrise.

"There it is, there it is," he yelled.

I saw the flash, but mostly my father's face and his brass buttons that seemed to glow red for one instant.

"That's how I came home to you, everybody. Just look at that power."

The cloud flowered, mushroomed, turned itself inside out, and poured into the sky. Red fire burned in the middle of browns and grays, colors that hid the red almost. But it was there—the fire burning at the center, the red fire that charred the North Wind's puffed cheeks and squeezed eyes until it blew itself away, trailing black smoke and its pride. It was there in the middle of the rising columns of earth and clouds boiling over, clouds bursting into clouds, whipping themselves inside out, changing colors over and over. Red, yellow, and black, colors from the fire. Gray, brown, and beige, sand from the desert floor, Daddy said.

And then the picture blurred at its edges, unfocused itself into other shapes—smoke arches, long floating strings, dots and dashes. In no time at all, everything floated away, on the jet stream, Daddy told us.

"I thought it would last longer," I said. "Won't they do it again?"

Daddy laughed, "It's time to go home now and get some hot breakfast. Wasn't that amazing, kids?"

Everyone who had gotten up to watch the blast talked about it in school that day. "Did you see it?" Our desert land had been chosen once again for an important government project.

The front page of that night's newspaper had pictures of the before and after—frame houses before, no frame houses after; dummied soldiers before, no recognizable dummies after. Surprised cattle lay flat out in the dead grass on their sides, their hair singed white on the up side. Yucca Flats. Frenchman Flats. Mercury Test Site. Household words.

"Nobody can get us now," my daddy said.

I don't think about it much, but sometimes when I punch my pillow for more fluff, ready to settle into sleep, the cloud mists into long red airy fingers over everything, reaching across the stark blue.

BIRD OF
PARADISE

A drum was beating that night as my family and I entered the elementary school gymnasium. Animal skins were stretched across a portion of hollowed-out tree, two flat brown hands pounding on their surface. Instantly, I felt my pulse and the drum beating together. I ran to the stage, pulled myself up on my toes, peered over the edge.

The drummer's feet were bare. White flowers were laced around his ankle. His knees were bare, too, and a cloth hung between his legs. When I saw his padded breasts quivering as he drummed, I averted my eyes to the bold black strokes on the cloth which hung from below his navel. How could he ever run or jump or move quickly, I wondered, in such a small square of material?

It reminded me of a few weeks before when my friend, Jackie, and I dared each other not to wear underpants to school. At recess, we challenged each other to somersault over the tricky bar under the slide. We both did lightning somersaults, but after the first rush of anxiety and after looking around the playground and realizing no one had noticed, I tried it again, more slowly.

"Phyllis," my father retrieved me with his big hand wrapping around mine. "It's time for the show to start."

"When will Sonny, Popo, and Liliuokalanimoa come out?"
"Very soon. Just be patient."

They'd turned sideways when they first entered our house with straw hats, orange cloth bags stenciled with palm fronds and geckos, arms as big as the elm-tree trunk in our front yard. They were bigger than the front door.

"Aloha," they'd said.

Steve and I stared up at them, amazed at the amount of flesh squeezed into the woman's muu-muu and the men's flowered shirts.

"Aloha," they said again. "We say aloha, you say aloha."

"Aloha," we answered in small whispers.

"I am Liliuokalanimoa," the woman said. "This is Popo, and this is Sonny." She bent over my younger brother, Steve, and kissed his cheek. Then she lifted me into her arms. "Fine lady," she said. She squeezed my biceps with her large fingers and rolled them like bits of leftover dough. "Chicken bones. Liliuokalanimoa feed you some pork."

I smelled her freshly washed hair, black loose loops caught up by two abalone combs. Large mother, the round earth, the scent of ocean near her ears. She squeezed the whole of me, and I felt the mountain of her as I curved around her, my brown shoes hanging mid-air.

"Aloha," my mother said, coming out of the kitchen with a flour sack dishtowel. I'd embroidered the girl on the towel who washed pots and pans. Red and blue thread for her plaid dress, an unnatural flesh-colored thread on her arms and legs. My mother wiped her hands and stretched one to Liliuokalanimoa.

"Aloha, Mrs. Nelson." Liliuokalanimoa's corpulent fingers tangled with my mother's narrow ones. "Call me Lily. This is Sonny and Popo."

Mother shook their hands and pointed to her arm where a watch would have been if she owned one. "Rehearsal. What time?"

"Seven o'clock. Sharp." Sonny laughed like he'd swallowed the sun and punched Popo in the arm.

"It's six now," Mother said. "We'd better have supper right away."

"Right away," Popo mimicked.

"Make yourself at home."

"Right away," Popo said.

They sank into the chairs and sofas, spilling over the sides, melting the cushions. "Little princess," said Liliuokalanimoa. I was still in her arms. "You stay with me."

I felt like a bird in a nest as she took my hands into hers and rubbed them together like fine sandpaper. She bent and wiggled each of the toes poking out of my sandals, talking to them individually, giving each a Hawaiian name—*Hawaiki. Kamehameha. Kahumanu.*

Lifting both my arms, she sang. "Fly, pretty bird. High over the ocean, fly." We soared above waves leaping back and forth on the disappearing shore. She was a broad-winged seabird calling into the wind. I tasted salt on my lips.

"Lovely bird." She put her arms around my rib cage and sheltered my thinness in her soft arms.

"Phyllis, take the boys to your room," my mother called from the kitchen, drenched in steam from the open kettle of noodles. "Liliuokalanimoa will sleep on the fold-out in your dad's office, but have her put her things in your room for now."

I slid from Liliuokalanimoa's lap and lifted her orange cloth bag from the floor. "Follow me," I said.

The great hunks of Polynesia lumbered down the hallway and into my room and immediately tested the mattress on Elaine's and my bed. They bounced like curious children as the empty space in our bedroom filled with Sonny, Popo, and Liliuokalanimoa, their belongings, and their laughter. These were the people we'd heard about for months in church flyers, Sacrament Meeting announcements, and telephone calls asking us to provide room and board. For three dollars per family, church members and townspeople could see flaming torches, leaping bodies, and grass skirts. *A new cultural experience*, the poster on the church's bulletin board announced.

"Tall grass," Popo giggled as he rubbed the top of Steve's crew-cut hair. "Means very important man. Takes many brains to grow such tall grass."

Steve tossed his reserve aside and climbed onto the bed. I followed suit. We tickled and dodged, dived into pillows, pushed Sonny and Popo off the bed, and then dared the forbidden—jumping on the mattress. As we flew, our hair flapped like wings, and Liliuokalanimoa made seabird sounds. And the seawind lifted us higher until we feared Mother might discover our serious crime.

So we nestled into Liliuokalanimoa's sides. She showed us how to make swimming fishes and ocean waves with our hands. "Talking hands," she said. "Tell stories to many people. One time, wind blow like mighty warrior. Coconuts fly like round birds. Trees bend to ground. Fishes swim to village to warn people. The bravest fish walks up and breathes fire onto man's foot, but no one listens."

"A fish breathing fire?" I asked, a large-eyed question.

"When fish breathes fire," Liliuokalanimoa continued, "everybody runs to hide. They know big trouble is coming." She formed fists in the air, dropped them from high to low, turned them into walking fish, then many people running. Her hands shifted like silky water.

I tried to make my own walking fish, but my fingers were awkward next to Liliuokalanimoa's.

"Dinner's almost ready," Mother called from the kitchen. "Phyllis. Your turn to set the table."

As I counted plates, utensils, and napkins, the oven started to smoke, the acrid smell of a burn on the elements. Mother opened the oven door and large fits of smoke burst like a volcano into the kitchen.

"Oh no," she almost cried, waving the smoke away with her hand. She lifted the scratched metal pan of bubbling cheese with the two matching pot holders I'd made at church in my Primary class called Larks. Larks, Bluebirds, and Seagulls for age nine-, ten-, and eleven-year-old girls. "Greet the day with a song," was our motto. "Serve gladly. Worship Heavenly Father, and make others happy." I'd cross-stitched it in primary colors on a brown linen sampler.

"Oh, thank goodness!" mother sighed with relief. "The casserole's okay. Don't forget the salt and pepper, Phyllis."

After everyone was seated around our table, Mother presented her famous Pot of Gold casserole—wide noodles, hamburger, cheese, canned corn, canned pimientos, bits of green pepper. And her homemade rolls with homemade apricot jam. And a bounteous tossed green salad. Liliuokalanimoa and Popo took small servings of the casserole, but when Popo passed it to Sonny, he shoveled half of it onto his plate. My mother looked at my father with carefully screened horror.

"Sonny," she said.

Sonny looked up eagerly.

"I see you like food," she stuttered.

"Very good luau," he said as he poured his second glass of milk and speared the salad leaves out of the serving bowl as if they were fish. He embraced every bite with true love. "You are beautiful mother of food. A pearl woman."

Slowly, my mother's mouth closed and her face softened. After all, she had her domestic pride. Biting back a smile, she blushed, said thank you very much, and hurried from the table to look at the clock.

"You're going to be late if you don't leave right this minute," she pretended to scold.

"No problem," Sonny said. "Hawaiian time is no time at all." He sat back in the chair, tipped it back against the wall which was forbidden in our household, and rubbed his massive stomach. "Pearl Woman makes beautiful dessert, I think."

Ice cream and Aunt Zenna's homemade brownies had been the originally planned menu, but just in case, Mother went to our storage closet for jars of preserved peaches and apricots. She had resources and bottles of pride; nobody would go hungry in her house.

After three servings of ice cream and one mason jar of peaches, Sonny leaned back again and patted his stomach like a best friend. "Beautiful lady, Mrs. Nelson. Beautiful cook. You make Sonny happy. You like gifts, Mrs. Nelson?"

My mother's elegant face softened into a young girl's shyness. I loved this girl who sometimes slipped from my exacting mother: vulnerable, holding out bare fingers to be touched, letting oyster shell colors escape from her fortress.

"A gift? For me?"

"Yes, beautiful mother."

And abruptly, Sonny picked himself up. "Lily. Popo. Let's go."

At seven forty-five they left for the seven o'clock rehearsal, no worry, no rush. Popo trailed after him with slow shuffling feet, and Liliuokalanimoa blew me a kiss before she lifted her bulk out of the kitchen and into the evening.

"Aloha," she said.

Luau, hula, coconut, lei, aloha. Steve, Elaine, and I repeated the new words to each other as we settled down for the night on the living room floor. We didn't mind the floor, especially when there was so much magic in those big bodies we awaited. We talked about the waves and the fire-breathing fish. We talked stories with our fingers and wrists.

"Do you remember *Bird of Paradise*?" I asked Elaine. "The movie where they sacrificed the chief's beautiful daughter?"

"Yes," she said sleepily.

"I remember," I said. A languid breeze nudged the grass walls of the hut I could see in the dark while exotic striped insects tiptoed past. "Don't you sometimes think you were a princess like that?"

"A princess," said Elaine out of the depths of her pillow, "but not a human sacrifice."

"A human sacrifice," I said. "What's that?"

"When somebody dies for somebody else."

"But what happens to the somebody else after the other somebody dies? Do things get better?"

"They're supposed to. Go to sleep, Phyllis. I'm tired."

And as I waited for sleep to come, I felt Liliuokalanimoa brushing my hair with her abalone combs and weaving stems of hibiscus into my hair. Wrapped in bright orange cotton woven with purple geckos, I heard drums calling me to the fire. And a torchbearer led us, me and Liliuokalanimoa, and we walked barefoot into the night and to the fire, our pulses captured by the drumbeat, our bodies prisoners to the unceasing rhythm. Slow, steady, stalking feet of rhythm walked through my blood, strode into my arms and my legs and my body. Firelit eyes glowed in the dark, watching, waiting for Liliuokalanimoa and Princess Phyllis in her coral-hued flowers.

Liliuokalanimoa took my hand and said the gods smiled on me. Her hand, my safety, my comfort, absorbed my fear as I faced all the anger the earth had ever known in the volcano's fury. And I stood straight and tall as Sonny and Popo led me to the lip of the fiery furnace. I told my people to stop crying, that I'd save them. And then I leapt off the edge into the next morning where I woke, happy to discover Liliuokalanimoa in the next room; no one had asked me to sacrifice anything for anybody; I was lying next to Steve and Elaine on army blankets on the floor; I could hear my mother and father talking quietly in the bathroom; it was morning and a new day and the volcano was quiet now, the sun in the sky.

Sonny ate eight eggs for breakfast. Sunny side up. Popo ate six, Liliuokalanimoa four. Mother made a triple batch of cinnamon rolls, and Sonny finished off a panful before they cooled down.

Though Mother smiled and played the gracious hostess, I could see her impatience growing. Her household budget had limits.

"I'm glad I don't have to provide for them all the time," I heard her mutter to my father when she cleared the table. "They remind me of threshers. This could add up."

Before I left for school, Liliuokalanimoa squeezed my arms again. "Little princess," she said. "You eat more. There are gods in the animals and in the mangoes. The gods come inside you when you eat their gifts."

"Liliuokalanimoa?" I asked. "Did you ever watch a chief's daughter jump into a volcano?"

"That's an old old story, Phyllis. Old old old."

"Did you ever think you might jump into the flames?"

"Every girl wonders."

"What's a human sacrifice?"

"Don't worry, small girl." She wrapped her arms around me as if I were a delicate gift of gold. She stroked my neck and rocked me like a new baby. I closed my eyes and stopped wondering about anything. Secure in her arms. I didn't want to walk out the door or go to school or run in the playground, slide down slides, swing, turn somersaults over the tricky bars. I wanted to stay in this ocean of arms, Liliuokalanimoa petting my cheek with one finger.

The Boulder City Elementary School gym had been imposingly gray in the dusk when we parked our car across the street, excitement riding high in my throat. *An Evening in Polynesia.* Torches were twisted into the front lawn. Elaine, Steve, Mom, Dad, and I had walked up the sidewalk past the flames, up the steps, into the brisk-looking hall, into the gymnasium where I'd sung in the shepherd choir at Christmastime and where our fifth-grade class sang "I'm Happy When I'm Hiking" at last month's PTA meeting. Nurses checked our hearing in this room; we'd rubbed our fingers into inkpads for a statewide fingerprinting project; we'd been given our paper-cup dose of Dr. Salk's miracle vaccine by smiling nurses.

But tonight, the gymnasium wasn't the gymnasium anymore. It was dark and filled with the beating of a steady drum. After my father retrieved me from the edge of the stage, we found a place on the second row. As I sat on the metal folding chair, I heard whispering grass skirts, swishing while people walked back and forth behind the burnt-orange curtain. The painted-on-butcher-paper palm trees someone had hung on the gymnasium walls seemed to sway in the dark. The walls moved away and folded into the night, and a volcano burned in the distance, way off in the direction of B Hill.

The curtains opened, and more drums joined in. Suddenly, Sonny, dressed in a loincloth, a torch in hand, leapt out of the wings, yelling like a fierce warrior. A line of men followed behind, Popo included, chugging across the stage with widely spaced flat feet, stabbing the air with their spears, and grunting words I'd never heard, words that weren't really words, but power. Sonny looked fierce and proud. Not the laughing, giggling Sonny who bounced on Elaine's and my bed. I scooted closer to my father for protection.

As the drummers' hands heated up, leaning more heavily into the stretched skin heads, warriors flew across the stage like winged beasts. The torch cast pulsing shadows on their gleaming bodies. The stage itself began to pulse. The gymnasium was the inside of a drum, and my heart was beating wildly. The women suddenly appeared, shaking their hips violently. Liliuokalanimoa wore a grass skirt, a cloth tight around her breasts, and a bold-colored wreath of flowers—white-tongued stamens thrusting out of waxy reds, purple cups to hold rainwater, and orange-petaled birds tipped with royal blues. She seemed a stranger to me, too, but then the mood changed, and she softened from an angry mountain to a floating seabird.

Ukeleles and guitars tempered the drumbeat; the women's hands talked to us gently. Their hips swayed like slow tide. Orchids in crowns, orchids fastened over ears, long black hair trailing over their shoulders, falling over their breasts, their long torsos bending slightly at the waist, except Liliuokalanimoa's torso was not so long as it was round and full and bounteous, a ring of flesh pouring out over the top of her grass skirt.

"They should have covered themselves more," my mother whispered to my father, looking anxiously at me and Steve, the youngest ones, to see how we were reacting to these bodies so sumptuously displayed in front of our eyes.

"Don't worry about it," my father whispered back. "That's how they do things in Hawaii."

"How do you know?" she said crossly, as if she'd heard this kind of response from him before, as if he made up answers to suit his convenience. "You like it, admit it." She nudged him with her elbow and folded her arms with semi-disgust.

"Let's everybody enjoy themselves," he said, taking my hand in his.

"Aloha," the performers shouted. When no one answered them back, they said it again. A few feeble voices answered.

"When we say aloha, you say *A-lo-ha!*"

"A-lo-ha!" the audience finally shouted back.

A parade of sizes and shapes, a chorus of ukeleles, a steel guitar, someone blowing a conch shell, an adoring couple singing "The Hawaiian Wedding Song" into a microphone. And then the drums heated up again and a sliver of a girl from Tahiti appeared on the stage, vibrating her hips as if they were a machine plugged into something. Hips couldn't go that fast, and then suddenly the whole stage was alive, everybody motoring around with some part of their bodies oscillating like crazy—their arms, their hips, their legs, their heads. Perspiration. The whole stage erupting like a volcano, the bodies delirious in its flames until they collapsed in a heap on the floor. I felt a sharp cramp in my hand.

I'd been holding my breath and squeezing my father's knuckles, working hard as I sat on my chair in the second row, caught by the tidal wave that swept over the edge of the stage and down onto the floor of the gymnasium of Boulder City Elementary School and swamped all of us sitting there. I released my father's sweating hand. He loosened his necktie. I felt wet everywhere. Islands. Oceans. Tides surprising me, catching me unaware.

"Aloha," the performers shouted. "Aloha," the audience roared back, a large ocean wave heaving back and forth from the stage to the audience. "Amazing." "Great show."

After five minutes of wild cheering, the audience finally gave up and began drifting away. Sonny leapt off the stage and searched through the dark until he found my mother, who was still sitting on her folding chair. "Pearl Woman. Stand up. A gift from me."

"What?" she said, her metal folding chair creaking as she shifted weight onto her feet and laughed nervously.

He slipped a lei of orchids over her head. Then he leaned close and put his arms around her shoulders. "Lovely mother. Queen of women."

His eyes were deep brown, and his black eyelashes were curled by nature. His chest was wet, wide, bare, brown, and strong, with the wet scent of deep sand. And he held my mother as he kissed her on the cheek.

I'll never forget that picture of her. Caught in his arms. Authority erased from her face, surprised before she could protest. Pleasure there. Forgetful of her role as our mother, one on one with Sonny, bare in front of us. A man and a woman, not my mother and Sonny. She closed her eyes when he kissed her and seemed to take a deep breath before she remembered us standing there watching. And then she laughed to dismiss him. "Oh, Sonny. You character! What am I going to do with you?"

"Beautiful lady." He touched her lips with his finger, his eyes burning black. "Shhh."

"Great show," my father said, reaching for Sonny's hand to shake it. Sonny took a last look into my mother's eyes, broke the embrace, shook hands, grinned, and began to giggle again, the Sonny we knew from the day he arrived and bounced on Elaine's and my bed.

I cried for three days when they left. I couldn't stop.

The morning after the show, Liliuokalanimoa held me in her lap again. She squeezed and hugged me, and I squeezed and hugged her back.

"It's time for school, Phyllis," my mother said. "You're almost late."

"I don't care," I said.

"But you have to care about school. That's the only way you'll ever learn anything."

"I don't want school." I pressed against Liliuokalanimoa's breasts and wrapped a loose strand of her hair in my fingers. "I'm Hawaiian."

"Come on, Phyllis." Mother pulled me out of Lily's arms, dragged my limp body across the floor, put me on the piano bench, put my shoes on my feet, and bent over to tie them. "Liliuokalanimoa, Sonny, and Popo have to go now. You don't want to make them sad."

"I'm going with them."

"But your teachers will miss you."

"I don't care. I go by Hawaiian time."

"What about me? I'd miss you. How would I get along without my little pianist? My happy girl who loves her Father in Heaven? I'll walk to school with you. Okay?"

"No."

Liliuokalanimoa walked over to the piano bench and knocked on my forehead with her knuckles. "You'll have a coconut head if you don't go to school. Empty when the milk dries up. Big sea turtle roll you out to sea."

"You want me to stay?" I asked, surprised.

"You belong here in this soil with your mama and papa. Some- day you can come to me, but your roots dry up if you go away now."

I looked at my feet, my long toes in my sandals, and imagined them crisp and brittle and blowing away.

"Good-bye, beautiful princess. When big volcano blows on my island, I call for you. You save my people. Aloha."

I dipped my chin to my chest to hide its quivering. "Aloha," I answered in a feeble voice.

"Good-bye, daughter of Pearl Woman." Sonny bent over my mother who still knelt, and over me who sat on the piano bench with legs dangling. He kissed our foreheads.

My mother looked at the floor. "I'll walk Phyllis to school, so I'll say good-bye for now."

"Car takes us away in five minutes. Fast away." Sonny's eyes were large shining mirrors.

"Listen for my call at night when everything's quiet," Liliuokalanimoa whispered in my ear. "Don't forget. You can come to me." She made the sound of the bird flying over the waves one last time.

And Mother and I went off to school, my heart an ancient sea turtle, heavy, slow, a shell of loneliness inside my ribs. Some bare brown feet had walked inside me, wiggled their toes, and left a major design.

Mother held my hand tightly. "I'll miss them, too," she said, and we didn't say anything else for three blocks, except I heard her swallow a whisper of "Aloha" while we waited for a car to pass on Wyoming Street.

AT THE
TALENT SHOW

Act I. The Soloists

When I was nine years old, the bishop of the Boulder City Ward, who happened to be my father, asked me to be the organist for Primary. Mormon children met together at Primary on Wednesday afternoons to study the restored gospel and sing such things as "The Handcart Song" about pioneers who walked across the plains singing "Some must push and some must pull."

"It's time to share the talent God gave you," my father said.

I said yes. I went to work. And, of course, I thought I sounded good. The teachers in Primary told me so; at the time I didn't understand how adults manipulated children, praising anything that wasn't total disaster.

Week after week, I listened for word filtering through the ward at large, hoping to hear about the new virtuoso rising up from under the desert sand, bubbling like a spring into the ward consciousness.

One Sunday afternoon at Sacrament Meeting, my father, in his position as bishop, made an announcement: "Two weeks from this Friday night, we're having a ward talent show. Dust off your banjos and ukeleles, warm up your vocal cords, mend that costume at the back of your closet. This is for the whole ward, not just for the few pros we love, but always hear from."

During the week, the verification I'd been waiting for came. I received three phone calls.

"Hello, dear. This is Sister Floyd. I've heard you're a fine little pianist. Could you accompany me for the talent show? I'd like to sing again."

Sister Floyd had six children who never sat still at church. The youngest threw themselves onto the floor in tantrums when they couldn't drink every cup in the sacrament tray. They grabbed handfuls of bread when they were only supposed to take one piece of the Saviour's flesh. Sister Floyd was the woman I studied after my father told me about sex during a Sunday afternoon dinner when I asked the question he couldn't avoid answering. "She does that?" I asked myself later at Sacrament Meeting when I saw her with a baby on her lap. "Him too?" Her husband seemed so much smaller than she was.

Second phone call: "Hello. This is Brother Frost. I come out to the ward once in a while. Maybe you remember me, maybe not. I used to play trumpet in a combo. Do you think we could practice together for this talent show?"

I remembered Brother Frost. He didn't come to church much, and I'd heard whispers about how he was a Jack Mormon and how he'd fallen. He scared me, a shadow at the edge of the ward activities while I'd been taught to hold my candle high and bright and in the middle of things. He looked like a frost giant—a tower of a man with blond wavy hair, a red-veined nose, and midnight-blue eyes with snowflake spokes around his irises. But I'd been given my talent by God, my parents reminded me often. It wasn't mine to hoard, and I should be generous with it, like Jesus holding out his hands to the lame and the diseased.

"I'd be happy to play for you," I said.

Brother Higginson sounded like Methuselah when he called. "It's time to get my violin out. Polish up something for the show." He'd been retired from the railroad for twenty years and lived with his son, the town barber.

I was flattered. Nine years old, and three adults called me to accompany them. I was surprised they hadn't called Sister Earl, the ward chorister, organist, choir director, and all-around leader of music.

Brother Higginson started our first rehearsal by sinking into the big cushions on our sofa and telling me about his railroad days in Washington State—how he used to tend coal and clean cows off catchers. He unlatched his worn case that was more cardboard than cover, put the violin under his chin, and began tuning the strings. "Give me an A," he kept saying, as though I hadn't heard him. He struggled out of his seat and hobbled across the space between the sofa and the piano while I played more As.

He shook when he walked; he shook when he handed me the piano music. He also shook when he played. His solo was a blur. "Darn strings," he kept saying as he played a vague rendition of "The Hot Canary." "Slip right out from under my fingers."

He tried for a while, but finally said he'd had enough. "You're a fine little sight reader, Phyllis." He patted my head. "You've got something we talk a lot about in the business. It's called promise."

His fingers trembled as he laid the violin to rest. "My beautiful friend." He stroked the varnished wood with one finger. "Sleep tight," he said as he closed the case.

Brother Frost came over next. "He's trying to make a comeback," Mother told me when she saw his car pull up in front of the house. She shook her head like she was in a world where things went slowly. "I hope this'll be good for him. Your dad's trying to help him back on his feet."

"When I used to play this tune, the girls'd line up for a city block." Brother Frost handed me the brand-new sheet music to "Cherry Pink and Apple Blossom White." "I had to drive in to Vegas to buy this." But we didn't get through the piece. He kept stopping and apologizing for his lip, never passing "It's cherry pink . . ." without strangling the tone. "Out of shape," he said. "Flabby. Sometimes I wish I'd a been smarter about a few things."

He blurted a B-flat into my living room. "Let's try it again."

Once he passed the "pink," he had trouble on the falling note which wouldn't land in tune.

"Damn, damn, damn," he said while his cheeks purpled. I could hear the distorted curses coming out of the bell end of his trumpet while I struggled to modulate to a new key.

"I'll get this if it's the last thing I do," he said, opening the spit valve and shaking his trumpet dry. "I'm gonna do it. Damn rights, I'm gonna do it." He pulled out the mouthpiece, dried it with green felt, and placed the pieces of his instrument in the gold velvet interior of his trumpet case.

"I like your rhumba rhythm," he said. "And the way you sight-read! I bet you'll play Carnegie Hall some day."

"What's that?"

"The place of all places in New York City. If you play Carnegie Hall, you've made it big time."

"Did you play there?" I asked.

He laughed. "I've never seen the front doors, child."

"I was a lead in *H.M.S. Pinafore*, Sister Floyd said when she came over to my house after school. "Parowan High School's musical. You should have heard the audience when I sang "Little Buttercup." She tucked her hands under her breasts and asked me to play up and down a five-note scale. "AH, ah, ah, ah, AH, ah, ah, ah, AH." We slid up a half step and repeated it again, up and again, up and again, until her voice disintegrated. "Sore throat," she said.

Then she handed me the battered sheet music of "Little Buttercup," the one she'd used in high school. I sight-read the introduction successfully, glided into the first few bars of her song, and then she stopped me with both hands waving. "This is too high for my mature voice. Do you think you could transpose it to a lower key?"

Suddenly, my ascending curve toward musical fame seemed

threatened. I didn't know what transpose meant, let alone know how to do it. Ground shifted under the piano bench and my feet. My vision of Carnegie Hall had been growing larger ever since Brother Frost came to practice. The Grecian columns, its brass doors with floral ornamentation, its thousand steps leading to the entry guarded by stone lions. This picture which had been vast in my young fantasies diminished to tiny doll-house dimensions in one flash of a second. One question. One word I didn't understand. Tiny Carnegie.

"Oh," she said after the protracted silence, "if it's too hard for you, we'll just get by."

"I'm sure it's not too hard," I protested. "It's just that. . . ."

"No, no, never mind." She dismissed the subject with finality while one of her children slid down her leg as if it were a firepole.

I wanted to tell her I'd learn to transpose. I could do whatever I set my mind to if she'd just give me time. I could do music. I knew how to figure things out. But she was swamped by four of her children, their running noses and untied shoelaces, before I could plead my case.

"I'll sing all the verses," she said as she buttoned a child's sweater. "And don't forget the ritardando at the end. We need a dramatic ending, like my high school coach taught me."

The night of the talent show, I dressed in a homemade green dress with plaid trim. My big sister Elaine pinned a matching plaid bow in my hair and told me I might be pretty someday. "Maybe . . ." she said, "if the earth's axis shifts."

Mother showed me how to make the toes of my brown shoes shine with a torn piece of my old baby blanket—a flannel strip of faded stars and moons. "Rub circles on the toe until you can see yourself smiling back."

"So you're going to be in the talent show tonight," my dad said through a veil of steam rising from the breaded pork chops.

"Fancy that. My little nine year old playing up a storm for the ward."

"Four times she's going to be in the talent show." Mother filled her glass with grape juice. "Singing in a trio with her girlfriends and accompanying several members of the ward. Ray Frost included," she said in a different tone of voice. "Was that your idea, Herm?"

"Shh," my father said. A quick, short "Shh" was meant for her ears, not ours.

"Three people asked me to accompany them, Dad," I said proudly. "And they didn't ask Sister Earl."

"Oh really?" my dad said quietly.

"Sister Floyd, Brother Frost, and Brother Higginson."

"Big deal," my sister Elaine said.

"You might consider," my dad unfolded the paper napkin onto his lap, "that Sister Earl was too busy. Did you think of that?"

"Herman!" my mother said sharply. "Why did you have to say that?"

" 'Pride goeth before the fall'; you know that."

"Well, that's true," my mother acquiesced, passing green peas and pearl onions flecked with dill. "But Phyllis is a fine accompanist, and I'm sure the people who called her recognize her ability."

I put my elbows on the table and stabbed my fork into a baked potato just unwrapped from its foil. Always right, father, mother, always right to stop trains in their tracks, trains chugging to somewhere, stop them quickly, suddenly, unavoidably, to remind them to be humble and not chug with too much bravado, not to make too much of any accomplishment lest the Lord take it away, lest the Lord frown, lest, lest, lest.

"I don't mean to take anything away," he said again, "but you know how easy it is to be puffed up with pride. It's not an attractive thing to see, Phyllis."

Bloated fish. I'd seen them. Dead. Floating on top of the rank water at the edge of Lake Mead. Smelling for miles. Full of maggots and flies and death. It wasn't attractive. My father was right about that.

When they announced Brother Higginson's name, the first to perform, I walked up the stage stairs with care. I didn't want to fall after what my father had said. I promised myself not to puff up with self-importance. I promised to float on top of God's gifts to me, not pretending to any superiority because of them, to remember I was only a lucky wayfarer who'd been given presents to carry to God's house, not to keep for myself.

Brother Higginson quivered like a butterfly wing all the way from his chair in the audience to his place on the stage. Everyone clapped when he arrived safely. Then he rested the violin against his chest and asked me for an A. Five, six, eleven times I played an A until he was satisfied. Slowly and shakily, he lifted the violin into playing position, the chin rest snug, his left arm extended uncertainly. His tremulous bow bounced lightly on top of the strings and made imprints of music on the silence. He nodded for me to begin the introduction, which I did. Pregnant silence as his bow hovered over the strings. Finally he stabbed at the high E which was supposed to sound like a canary whistling, but he hadn't aimed right. We started over three times, and finally he stepped out of playing position and said to the audience: "Do you remember the one about the train conductor in Walla Walla?"

After that, no one paid much attention to his "Hot Canary." They thought it was just another joke. I heard myself laughing with them, laughing so breezily at this man, God's butterfly. Yet the sound of my laughter burned my ears, and I worried about pride even though Brother Higginson was genuinely funny as he stood there laughing at himself and shaking like he was without a coat in the Arctic.

Sister Floyd was dressed in a yellow checked pinafore over

a white lacy blouse. She'd painted two bonbons of pink on her
cheeks and tied a yellow satin bow around her neck. Her youngest children slid off their wooden folding chairs and wandered in
the aisle until several of the sisters in the audience coaxed them
into their laps and secured them with their arms.

Sister Floyd had told me to wait until she gave me the go-
ahead. She needed to take a few deep breaths and find the most
comfortable place to stand. She swayed where she stood, back and
forth as if she were rocking a baby to sleep, and she closed her
eyes to concentrate on the words and music that would soon be
coming out of her mouth. Finally, she looked at me and mouthed
the word, "Okay."

"I'm called Little Buttercup, dear Little Buttercup." First, she
leaned toward the audience on her right side, then on her left.
When she sang "Sailors should never be shy," she wagged her finger like a coquette, turned her back to the audience, and peeked
over her shoulder to flutter her eyelashes. Everybody laughed and
cheered. "Mommy, Mommy," her smallest boy shouted.

"I've snuff and tobaccky, and excellent jacky." Everybody joined
in the fun, and there was so much noise that nobody heard her
shrill notes that were out of tune. Nobody but me noticed when
she started singing an octave lower.

"Yeah, Sister Floyd," everybody cheered when she curtsied at
the end. "Yeah," as if she'd hit a home run.

As he came to the stage, I noticed that Brother Frost wore a
too-starched, short-sleeved shirt, a light-blue tie, and slacks that
matched his eyes. He was so tall he had to stoop under the valance
that fell in graceful pleats from the top of the stage. His trumpet
looked small under his arm, like a plastic toy for boys. He looked
more like an uncomfortable giant than a trumpet player, and I
wondered how he ever picked up his first horn and decided to
make music.

When this great hulking man put this instrument to his lips, everyone in the audience looked at him curiously. Who was he? Where had he come from? But then I spotted my father beaming from his place in the audience and remembered he had something to do with Brother Frost standing on the stage with a brass horn in front of the congregation of the Boulder City Ward.

Brother Frost took a huge gulp of air, like Jacob at the bottom of his ladder, deciding whether or not to begin the ascent to heaven. Then came the notes: "It's cherry pink" almost in tune until he slid off the highest one. But he didn't stop to apologize like he had in rehearsal. Not then. Not later when he came to the same hurdle in the piece. He was perspiring, great large blotches of wet diluting the starch in his shirt, trickles of water down his temples. He pushed the notes through the brass as if he were making a bid for a new chance.

When he finished, the audience clapped with polite warmth, but my father stood up and cheered, clapped his hands hard, even whistled between his teeth, and time stretched until all I could hear was the sound of one man clapping. I wanted to close my eyes and ears to my father, embarrassing me as he stood there by himself, clapping for Brother Frost who wasn't all that good on the trumpet, clapping even though the rest of the audience had stopped.

Brother Frost shrugged his shoulders, rubbed the top of my head, and whispered, "Doesn't matter about every note. We made it all the way through, didn't we?"

He was smiling, but his lips were blue, his nose red. The frost giant's hand on my head was freezing cold even though he was covered with perspiration. The chill filtered through my curls and into my skull.

I felt two sensations as I walked off the stage: an indiscriminate one related to the harsh tones in Sister Floyd's voice, the liver-spotted hand curving around the neck of Brother Higginson's violin, Brother Frost's cold hands, my father standing alone in the audience, and his words about pride; the other was a sense of rare coldness in the Boulder City Ward in the desert in Nevada. Like words and snow falling on our heads as we tried to sing and play. Little people in a giant snowstorm, walking through white, hidden by a thick curtain of flakes. Potential stars trying to shine in the broad daylight and in the snow. The snow piling high, lulling everyone to sleep beneath its blanket. When we open our mouths in our dreams to sing pure high notes, to purse our lips on a brass mouthpiece, or to steady our bow hand, more snow falls. Our tongues and our mouths and my hands slow in the cold. The sound freezes.

Act II. The Three Chiquitas

I scanned the audience to find my two best friends, Jackie and Sheila, but the chairs next to them were taken. I'd been up on the stage too long. Choosing the next best alternative, I headed to the row where my family was sitting. My father wasn't there, though. Neither was my mother. But Elaine and Steve were. I scooted in next to them.

"Where'd Mom and Dad go?" I asked Elaine.

"They're helping one of the performers," she said, cracking her chewing gum between her molars.

"Can I have some gum?"

"Most certainly not," she said as she always did, as if she was the Queen of Something while I was but a serf.

"Don't sit so close to me." She pushed me away with her elbow.

I wanted to ask her if she thought I'd played the piano well or if she thought I'd go to Carnegie Hall someday, but I knew the answer before I asked the question.

"Come here, Steve," I said to my four-year-old brother. "Come sit with me." I herded him into my lap and held him tightly while

Brother Hamlin played a polka on his clarinet. I needed somebody close to me. I needed Steve's heartbeat under my hand.

"Do you love me?" I whispered in his ear.

He nodded yes, my faithful brother.

"Did you like how I played the piano?"

He nodded yes again.

"Are you always going to be my best friend? Through thick and thin and cold and dark and dreary?"

"Yes," he whispered back. I squeezed him and kissed his rubbery cheek.

Then I felt a finger tapping my shoulder blade. It was Jackie. "Phyllis, it's time. We have three performers until we're on."

"Already?"

At Sister Earl's urging, Jackie, Sheila, and I had decided to form a trio and sing "Chiquita Banana." We hadn't practiced all that much, spending more of our time buying plastic bananas, grapes with rubber stems, and strawberry pincushions at the dime store; testing ways to tie scarves on our heads—knots low on our foreheads, knots above our bangs, knots over the right and left ear, under the chin, at the back of our necks; experimenting with makeup—corals, reds, pinks on our cheeks and lips, blues, greens, grays on our eyes—what would look best on stage, what would make us glow; figuring out a way to make the bananas, grapes, and strawberries stay securely on our heads—giant safety pins, glue, tape, needle and thread, earmuff headpieces without the muffs; deciding on the look-alike white blouses and orange squaw skirts that we were supposed to wash, put on a broom handle while wet, and fasten with rubber bands to dry, the latest fashion in town. Last of all, we practiced our song.

"Come on," said Jackie.

Even though we'd been preparing for weeks, I didn't feel like singing yet. I wasn't feeling warm enough to sing about bananas and the equator and still needed Steve against my chest and my

arms tight around him. But when Jackie and Sheila started backstage without me, I slipped Steve off my lap, told him to go back
to his seat. "This will be *uno* great act," I told him in my best
señorita imitation.

"Sure," Elaine said. One last elbow in my rib. "Don't buy her
propaganda, Steve."

In the girls' bathroom, Jackie unlatched her mother's brown
vinyl cosmetic case and placed bottles and tubes in a row on the
sink. She opened a plastic square of rouge and spread large red
balls on her cheeks, bright unnatural spots that seemed to keep
growing, even after her fingers had gone to other tasks. Sheila
opened a Baroque Pink lipstick, its tip sculpted into a fragile peak
from much use. I unscrewed the lid of Peacock Blue eye shadow
and smudged my eyelids. This was the real thing, our first official time to wear makeup for public display. I was shivering as if
caught in the uncertain sails of Columbus's ship as he set off for
the edge of the world.

Jackie manifested some natural artistic ability as she painted a
new face on her old one, but Sheila knew the territory as if she
had been born with makeup in her hand. She looked more beautiful than seemed possible as she lined her eyes with brown pencil
and made her lips stand up in peaks.

I pressed a tube of lipstick against my mouth, dark red, bold
red, a gash on my face because I couldn't follow the outline of
my slippery lips, not enough experience in my wrist. Dark blue
on the eyelids, smeared heavily from brow to lashes, me peering
through two holes in a deep blue sea, eyes blinking slowly under
the painted heaviness of the lids. Red on my cheeks—wide circles
of paint. Egg-colored powder on my nose and forehead. The ban-
danna tied in place, knot on top of my head. Bananas, grapes,
and strawberries dangling over my ear. Giggling all the way to the
stage in our white blouses and orange squaw skirts. Jackie Jewel,
Sheila Shimmer, Phyllis Phenomenal, we'd named ourselves.

Sister Earl smiled as she sat down on the piano bench where I'd been a few minutes ago, probably suspecting what was to follow. Nevertheless, she thumped out the bright calypso rhythm on the piano. We placed our hands on our hips as we'd planned, then bounced with the rhythm.

"I'm Chiquita Banana," we started out strongly, "and I've come to say." Laughter from the audience, then a titter from Jackie. We all looked straight ahead, steeling ourselves against the inevitable.

"Bananas have to ripen in a certain way." More laughter from the audience. Because I never had been able to keep a straight face when anybody laughed at one of my jokes, I was the next to go, and the entire house of cards went with me. Laughter engulfed us, took us for a ride, wouldn't let us stay at the talent show. Soon we were bending over, our hands on our knees, our mouths wrenched out of shape with laughter, our sides being pressed by the sides of our arms in an attempt at quiet, at peace, at containment; the show must go on.

Between us, we popped out a few words here and there, sometimes completing an entire phrase. "Chiquita, Chiquita," somebody called out of the audience. "*Ariba*," plus a high trill on someone's tongue. Everyone seemed to be having a good time, laughing along with us, no investment in perfection. Perfection was whatever happened at the Boulder City Ward Talent Show.

Somehow, we rallied at the end, just soon enough to lend credibility to the fact we'd come on stage to sing a song.

"So, you should never put bananas. . . ." We climbed the scale up to the high point of "nas." We hit the high D together, bravely suppressing our laughter. Together, we held the final high note in a triumph of unity, clarity, and song. Jackie Jewel, Sheila Shimmer, Phyllis Phenomenal—flourishing our arms in front of the ward, bobbing the fake fruit on our heads, flaunting our innocence, our preadolescence, our tight buds of femininity soon to blossom. The Three Chiquitas.

After the high D, we finished off with the sermon from the United Fruit Company: (Where should you never put bananas?) "In the refrigerator. No, no, no, no." We shook our hips and fingers in a scolding fashion and then hissed the words "cha, cha, cha" like sassy Latinas. The applause was wide and large and plentiful.

We were a hit. We'd laughed, sung a little, blushed much, paraded ourselves in front of the audience.

And I stood there and bought their applause, swallowed it; I stood there in the swell, my body growing taller, smarter, brighter, nourished by the sound, swelling with the helium of praise, and warming my toes, my heels, my knees, thighs, and chest. They loved us. They loved me. This was much more fun than being an accompanist or playing a piano solo while everyone squirmed and coughed and wished I'd hurry up and finish. This was the applause that spoke to me.

I knew I was destined for something larger. The lights out there somewhere were waiting for my particular beauty, talent, élan. Waiting for all of us—Sheila Shimmer, Jackie Jewel, Phyllis Phenomenal. But especially Phyllis Phenomenal who played the piano too and could sight-read like lightning.

Act III. Lovely Hula Hands

When Jackie, Sheila, and I descended the stairs on our way to the bathroom to change out of our costumes, I saw something I wasn't sure I saw. Someone who looked like my father climbing up the stairs, climbing up to the stage, passing us as we climbed down.

He was dressed in a grass skirt, two half coconuts connected by a string hanging around his neck and covering his nipples, a few straggling hairs at the center of his chest, a sultry black wig on his head, red on his cheeks and lips, blue eye shadow like the blue on my eyes. My mother stood at the bottom of the stairs laughing, her hand over her mouth, the hem of her red and white jersey dress bouncing from her laughter. She had a handful of make-up—lipstick, rouge, eye pencils. She must have been the artist who painted the man who just brushed my side. My father.

"Let's go sit out front," Mother said. "Hurry." She pushed me along. "You don't want to miss this."

"What's happening?" I said.

"Stop asking questions."

She put her arm around my shoulders, and we walked through the room that usually served as a classroom, now doubling as a dressing room, prop room, all-purpose throw-everything-in-there room. Music cases against the wall; Maori sticks that had been tossed back and forth by a former New Zealand missionary and his wife while they chanted a Maori song; Brother Jeppson's magic act—a top hat, a cane, a white rabbit in a small cage; a pair of stilts; a Spanish dancing costume hanging from a nail where a picture of Joseph Smith receiving his vision hung on Sundays. We walked around the obstacles and opened the door onto the large room where everyone was watching my father, who usually appeared before them in a suit and tie on Sundays.

The music was beginning. Ukeleles. The sound of the Pacific. Water crashing into shores, rolling out. Mother and I stood against the wall because our seats had been taken by someone's children. Mother could hardly contain herself, wrapping herself with her arms, hugging them tightly around her so her bursting insides wouldn't fall out in front of everyone.

I'd seen my father at home. He loved to dance, and it often seemed to me that some part of him could only be released when music played. And now he was swiveling his hips, paddling air with his arms on one side of his body and then the other.

Without his eyeglasses, his eyes were soft blue and inviting like movie star eyes. Bedroom eyes, like Elaine told me she had. Pretty face. Soft skin on his chest. Delicate fingers. His lustrous lashes that mother had mascaraed black fanned out against the backdrop of his painted blue eyelids. He had long black hair in place of a long blank forehead. He wore a flower in his hair and colored leis piled over his shoulders. And I wondered where he learned to make his hands swim like fish through the water and his fingers scoop for poi.

A scratchy version of "A Little Grass Shack in Hawaii" played on the ward's record player as he threw kisses to the audience, tossed his long tresses with one hand, shimmied the coconuts on his chest. My mother was laughing so hard tears were running down her cheeks.

I was not laughing yet because I was still too curious. My father maintained a solid deadpan: a disdainful island princess ignoring her suitors. He held his chin high as if to snub us and puckered his lips as if to say, "Kiss me, if you dare." And he arced the wrists of his "Lovely Hula Hands" more gracefully than a bird in motion. Wrists bending in and out, swan's neck hands. And then he started jutting his hips out faster, holding his arms wide, come-a, come-a.

Laughter raged like fire through the audience and swept over me. I couldn't hold back any longer. I laughed until tears rolled out of my eyes and my legs felt weak. My father, the dancer, the joker, the bishop of the ward.

Finally the music ended and he curtsied, his foot crossing in front of his bent leg rather than in back like in a proper curtsy, showing off the plastic leis around his ankles one last time.

A standing ovation. Two people standing up on their chairs and cheering. Whistles. Clapping hands, stamping feet sounding through the cracks of the ward windows into the night, passersby probably wondering what was happening inside.

"That's the funniest thing I've ever seen," I heard Sister Gibson telling my mother. "I swear it's the funniest."

"How'd you get your husband to do that?" someone asked.

"It was his idea," my mother said.

"Bishop Nelson should be a stand-up comedian," all these voices over my head, talking to my mother, spewing words about my father. "He's as good as any comic I ever saw." And I could hear their voices as they turned away from my mother, still talking. "He really looked pretty, didn't he? Even beautiful."

And I ran back through the room with the costumes and props. I ran onto the stage to hug my father and squeeze him with pride before he changed into his suit. Everybody loved my father.

As I hugged his hips covered with the grass skirt and as he stroked my cheek and everyone crowded around him to tell him he was sensational, I sensed I was hugging a mystery, even a trickster like Loki in the Norse myths my teacher read to us at school. Loki could change into anything, even a mare who birthed an eight-legged pony. I liked that my father was a surprise, but I needed to hold onto him for now.

"I love you, Daddy," I said while people pressed close to us.

"Did you like that?" he asked, beaming through the blue eye shadow, his powder, his rouge.

I looked up to tell him yes, yes, yes.

He wasn't talking to me. He was tossing words in the air over my head. Catching Sister Earl's words in return. "Definitely yes," she was saying.

"You really liked it?" he asked again.

I watched his face. His mouth was open in anticipation of her words. He was smiling, waiting, yet I could see him attempting to mask his eagerness. He didn't want Sister Earl to know it mattered; he didn't want himself to know it mattered. He was preening, tail feathers alive. He was puffing up before my eyes.

"Terrific. Just terrific," Sister Earl was saying. "Never saw anything so funny. I swear, Herman, you ought to get a job in Vegas."

He patted my head as he smiled with satisfaction. Then, as if I were something he wished were in another room, he whispered, "Don't hang on so tight, Phyllis," he said. "I'm sweating like a dog."

Sister Earl overheard. "Ladies don't sweat," she said. "They perspire."

"Guess I'm still a man, then." He laughed.

"You're one heck of a great guy." Sister Earl patted his shoulder, straightened his loops of leis, and kissed him on the cheek. My father shone like noon sun; he stood tall like the wooden Indian in front of the town drugstore. No war bonnet, but a high, proud chest and a black wig.

Then Sister Earl bent down and held my chin with two fingers. "Phyllis," she said. "Your dad was right. You do a great job accompanying. Glad I recommended you." Then she went over to the piano to close it up for the night.

Suddenly, I felt the weight of the bananas, grapes, and strawberries on my head.

"Let's go, Phyllis," my father said absentmindedly as if his cup wasn't full yet, looking around to see if anyone else waited to say something.

"Not yet, Dad," I said, still hanging onto his hips. "I need to ask you something."

"Come on, come on," he said, pulling me apart from him. "I've got to get out of this itchy skirt. Driving me bananas."

"I'm Chiquita Banana," I started to sing as we walked toward the stairs, "and I've come to say. . . ."

"How'd your song go?"

"We laughed too much."

"You can never laugh too much," he said as he pulled a flower out of his wig.

"Or dance too much?" I asked him.

"Right. By the way, you did a fine job helping out Brother Frost tonight. Appreciate your helping him out, getting him over the rough spots."

Suddenly, I summoned my courage and blocked the doorway to the stairs and the dressing room. "Do adults rule the world?"

"What do you mean?" He pulled the wig off his head and bent down on his haunches, his coconuts knocking against each other, until we were eye to eye. His blue eye shadow looked severe at close range.

"Sister Earl told all those people to call me, didn't she?"

"If you have to know, yes, she did."

"Nobody called me just because they thought I was good, did they?"

"That's extreme."

"And you told Sister Earl to tell them, didn't you?"

"You got to perform didn't you?"

"It's not the same." I stomped the stage with one foot. "Now I feel stupid, stupid, stupid! I wish I'd never learned to play the dumb piano."

"Come on, Phyllis. Settle down."

"And don't start preaching pride to me. You liked how everyone told you how great you were tonight. I watched you. You like being a star for yourself, not just for God. You can't fool me."

His grass skirt rustled in a draft that seeped through the wood frame of the Boulder City Ward house into the room where everyone's props were waiting to be taken home and put back in closets. And it seeped into me and my father's suddenly sad eyes as he excused himself. "I've got to change clothes," he said. "Wait for me."

SKETCHES FROM THE KEYBOARD

Cantilena

Con rubato   Op. 1, No. 1

*J*f I try to remember how the idea of culture began in my mind, I could mention a thick black seventy-eight–rpm recording of *Peter and the Wolf*. Mother announced it was composed by Sergey Prokofiev, a child of the Ukraine, only a few years before we were born in Boulder City, Nevada.

Elaine, Steve, and I played it on a red, kidney-shaped phonograph that had happy children decalled on its sides and a cord too short to reach the sofa's end table. We set the phonograph on the floor, threaded the cord underneath the sofa, and sent Steve, who was much like a young narrow worm, to retrieve the snaking plug and connect it to the wall socket.

After he emerged and one of us set the needle in the first groove, we draped ourselves on the pale green couch upholstered with a nubby fabric that burned our skin raw if we rubbed against it too hard, which we sometimes did as we listened to Peter trudging through the deep snow in the dark woods, Elaine, Steve, and I flat on our stomachs, leaning intensely into our elbows while we waited for the little bird to warn Peter. Hurry, Peter! Watch out! The Wolf!

Or I could talk about the Sunday afternoons after our family

came home from the Boulder City Ward house where we'd been
to Sacrament Meeting and partaken of the crumbled bread and
thimble cups of water. After we finished the pot roast dinner
Mother baked at 275 degrees in the oven all day, and after we
washed and dried the dishes, Mother tuned to a particular place
on the radio dial where Frank Knight would be introducing the
Longine Symphonette and the great classics. Elaine and I sometimes lounged on the green sofa in our underslips to beat the heat,
and our father always scolded us for being so immodest while our
mother chimed in with a similar opinion.

I do remember that in Boulder City, Nevada, in our white stucco
house with green shutters, with its sandy backyard where rattle-
snakes sometimes slithered, where Mother planted peach and
apricot trees that looked like sticks, where we hung out wet clothes
that turned into boards under the blast of the desert sun, our parents made a concerted effort to give us more culture than they'd
been given. They wanted us to have something they couldn't have
when they were young. They said that more than once.

But if I had to choose the most long-lasting impression regard-
ing culture, it wouldn't be the artificial insemination of recorded
music or music lessons which, in some sense, are like the decals
of the happy children on the phonograph: colored, plastered on,
glued to make a finished product, but only embellishments in the
end, never a part of the real machine. It would be the memory of
my mother's beautiful, clear, Idaho farm-girl voice and the fact
that she didn't believe in it.

When she was young and impressionable and lived on a failing
dry farm in southeast Idaho with her nine brothers and sisters, my
mother was told by her mother that Aunt Lois was the one with
talent. "We can afford voice lessons for only one of you," Grandma
told her, "and we've decided it should be Lois. Even then, I'll
have to stretch my egg money to pay the teacher. Maybe someday
there'll be enough for you. Meanwhile, count your blessings."

Twice I watched my mother try to sing a solo at a church meeting. An unflinching believer in the restored gospel and a lioness of God who would lead a charge for the cause of righteousness if necessary, she stood on the small wooden stage in the ward house and tied knots in her handkerchief as she waited for the pianist to finish the introduction. She stood there terrified, her heartbeat filling my ears, her butterflies migrating to my sympathetic nervous system. Then, she commenced with so much bravado that she made it through the first few lines. However, she seemed to become aware she was breaking some invisible contract with her all-knowing mother, who declared Lois *the* singer. This memory broke her will. Her voice shook at the edge of the tone, then cracked all the way to the end of the song.

The second time it happened, she didn't wait for my father who was bishop of the ward and had church duties to finish. She herded us children out of the building in a hurry, walked us home at a fast pace, and closed her bedroom door quietly. I knocked after time passed. "Mom?"

"I'll be out in a minute," she said.

"I think you're a beautiful singer," I said, my ear flat against the painted door. No sound at all. "You can sing 'Heavenly Aida,'" I whispered. "Remember?"

After the soft silence of quilts being lifted and slippers filled, she opened the door. The room was dark, the blinds closed. She pulled me to her soft stomach before I could see her face. "My little Phyllis." Her voice thick and unfamiliar, she patted my mass of curls. "This week, there's going to be a surprise for you. You just wait and see."

I lifted my arms to her waist and snuggled into the pillow of my mother. "What is it, Mama?"

"A surprise."

A few days later, a bulky, secondhand upright piano arrived. It came to our small house at the edge of town, not far from

B Hill with its whitewashed *B* and scurrying horned toads. It had a decorative mirror screwed into its cut-back top and was so heavy that four men grunted and complained about their backs the whole time they squeezed through our front door which had to be taken off its hinges. That tall, massive piano immediately became my mother's prize possession. She shined and polished it, then crowned it Queen of the Living Room with a miniature plaster of paris bust of Beethoven.

"You're all going to have piano lessons," she said proudly. "Every single one of you. Your Dad has agreed to sell extra insurance policies to make this possible. I've arranged for two different teachers for you girls to avoid competition. Steve, you'll get your chance when you're older." She rubbed a smudge from the piano's surface with the corner of her apron and turned Beethoven's statue to watch over whoever would be the first to practice.

Elaine's piano teacher was Mrs. Curry. I was sent to Mrs. Bourne. She placed my finger on a key and said, "This is middle C, the middle of the piano. You can always find it by looking for the two black keys. Remember, there are sets of two and sets of three."

I enjoyed finding the two black keys with middle C at their side, maybe responding to the romanticism of black keys raised above white ones—mountains stark against valleys which gathered dust. Elaine, however, responded to a different kind of romance.

Being older, pretty, and the possessor of bedroom eyes she often reminded me she had and I didn't, Elaine discovered boys about the same time she started piano lessons. I noticed her giving more meticulous attention to the dresses she wore and the makeup she applied to her face than she did to practicing her lessons. What was so great about squawk-voiced, spitting boys who wore their pants pachuco style? And all of a sudden, she was telling me not to be such a goody-goody piano practicer, to stay out of the bathroom when she was in there, out of her closet, out of her diary, her life. No exceptions.

This sudden severance of familial ties left me with more time to practice, though I actually liked the task. I liked when a piece came together, when it made sense and its logic revealed itself. But maybe I liked it because it was to my advantage, not because I was intrinsically more refined than Elaine, a fact I so much wanted to believe after she banned me from her territory. Mother often said, "If you'll practice, I'll do the dishes." At times she'd hold me and hug me and say, "You play so beautifully. What a wonderful girl you are." And sometimes she'd say, in serious tones, "When a boy thinks of marrying, he'll want a girl who can play the piano." I thought about that. If I had no striking physical attributes, as Elaine never ceased to inform me and I'd begun to believe, then I'd better hedge my bets for the future.

Whatever it was that motivated me, I proved quite proficient at the keyboard, especially at sight-reading. In fact, I became something of a showpiece at school, at church, and especially at home when the relatives dropped by. Instead of standing on my head or doing a cartwheel or showing them my new dress or a missing tooth, I was asked by my mother to play a "little number" for the aunts and uncles who really didn't want to hear their niece play, who would rather talk about what their own daughters or sons were doing, and I could feel them not wanting to listen, not wanting to offend my mother, not wanting to wait until I finished my piece of music. I actually timed them once, betting they wouldn't make it past the tenth measure of "Für Elise."

"Did you know Diane won student council representative for the freshman class, and Barbara Jean's going to Girls' State in Reno?" Aunt Grace said, before cue on the eighth measure. "The American Legion wants to sponsor her."

"Let's hear the rest of Phyllis's piece," Uncle Tommy said. He was always following behind his wife Grace like a dustpan, trying to gather the particles of hurt he knew his brothers and sisters sometimes felt. But Grace knew how to outwit him with her quick-draw tongue and sharpened survival skills.

"Isn't Phyllis a doll?" Grace said. "Such a smart young thing! Our kids are really something, aren't they? You just won't believe what Diane's teacher said about her essay."

The other aunts and uncles were also outmaneuvered by Aunt Grace. They could never tell stories to match, never have shining example children like hers.

I started to rebel when my mother wanted me to play the piano for them. "Please," she'd beg, but I could feel too many things going on in the room. I knew Uncle Elwin and Aunt Raity were embarrassed about their daughter who'd run away to Elko with a garage mechanic and come back asking for a place to stay. I knew Aunt Grace didn't like any of her brag time preempted, that she thought of our family as ragtag upstarts just off the edge of respectability because of our farm-girl mother from Idaho. My mother had been captain of the girls' basketball team of other farm girls while the town girls sat on the bleachers and gazed at their compact mirrors. My mother worked at Woolworth's for eighteen cents an hour so she could live in town and finish high school, even though she'd fought with her father, who insisted she was needed for the hens and butter and warned against the town riff-raff. My mother cried once when she told me about the three books her parents owned when she was growing up, my mother, hungry for culture. And mother kept being set aside by Aunt Grace and her stories about Barbara Jean and Diane who both won the Veterans of Foreign Wars' Essay Competition on "Why I Love America," in consecutive years no less.

"Please play the piano, Phyllis. Please." There was more than a request in my mother's voice, so I'd give in to that, but when I chose the classical pieces I'd worked so hard to perfect, I cut out the repeats and sped up the legato so I wouldn't feel the squirming start out there, behind my back, on the sofas and chairs. I could always feel the squirming. Even my dad's. He could take culture, but not if the timing was off. He knew about timing. "Why don't you play 'Tico Tico'?" he always asked. "People love to hear that. It's snappy."

Meanwhile, Mrs. Bourne planned a piano recital with a new twist. Instead of using her home for the event, as she usually did, she rented a building with a stage. Then, to make it more endurable for both the students and the parents who yawned every time they crossed another budding pianist's name off their mimeographed program, she asked the mothers to make costumes to match the songs their children would perform.

My classical piece was a sonatina by Clementi, my popular piece, "Frosty, the Snowman." Because a sonatina was hard to fabricate, my mother decided on a snowman suit. She cut old sheets with pinking shears, sewed the seams, made armholes and large cardboard buttons, and when the time came, stuffed the costume with gift wrap tissue.

Theoretically, this was a good idea, especially when she first crinkled the tissue and filled the cavity between me and the suit. But when I sat down on the wooden folding chair, which I needed to do to make it through the recital until my turn to play, the crisp, energetic tissue lost any body it ever had. When my turn came to perform, the tissue had settled to the bottom, and my suit was long and thin, except for the bottom, which sagged like a wet diaper. My stovepipe hat made of a poster paper cylinder and a scotch-taped rim, had deteriorated, too. It sagged over my eye as I minced across the stage, trying to keep the tissue paper from falling through the hole at the bottom, holding the snowperson illusion together with my thin arms.

I needed a blizzard that day, some kind of snowstorm in which to hide. Instead, I had to remember which key it was that started my piece.

The white keys all looked the same, almost as if they were covered with the snow I'd wished for. I finally picked middle C, no, not right, then F and then G; my knees started to shake. And then the storm I'd wished for seemed to come over me—a double-whammy storm, snow flurries everywhere, snow blinding me. I couldn't see anything. I was lost.

Like a nagging whisper in the night, I heard Mrs. Bourne's voice calling to me, as if she'd been calling to me for a long time. "D, Phyllis. Start on D."

D, beautiful D. I found it and caressed it. A marker in the storm. I almost laughed out loud as I rushed into the piece I knew so well. Even though my fingers were frozen into bulky stems by then, I forged my way as fast as I could to the final chord and stood up to take my bow as I'd been coached to do. A few pieces of tissue chunked to the floor. I kicked one with the toe of my shoe, then ran off the stage and started for the bathroom to shed the last vestiges of my snowman suit.

But Mrs. Bourne called me back on stage. "I want you all to know," she announced, "I've chosen Phyllis Nelson as the student who has made the most progress the past six months. I'd like to give her *A Golden Book of Beloved Hymns* in remembrance of this honor. We're proud of Phyllis." Mrs. Bourne's hand rubbed the curls on my head, and then she handed me the book with an angel gazing toward heaven on the cover.

Uncle Tommy, in his blue suit, yellow tie, and slick black hair, found me afterward and put his arms around me. "Phyllis, I'm real proud of you for hanging with it. I'm a musician, you know, and that's one of the most important things you can learn. Staying with it! Real proud of you, hon." Aunt Grace started to say something, but Uncle Tommy stuck out his hand to put her on hold.

My mother came up to me, shaking her head, and started pulling tissue out of the suit, hand over hand. She wiped the corner of her eye with one of the crumpled pieces. "What an idiotic idea," she kept saying. "A recital's not a costume party." She seemed to be talking to herself, not to me or Uncle Tommy or Aunt Grace. "My Phyllis. . . ."

"See you later, kid-do," Uncle Tommy said, nudging Aunt

Grace at the elbows to guide her toward the door. Then he leaned over and whispered into Mother's ear, something I couldn't hear.

"My little girl," I heard her whisper back as if she hadn't heard what he said either, as if she were the only person in the room.

Etude

Allegro, sempre legato   Op. 1, No. 2

Mother told me Mrs. Ramsey would be my new piano teacher. She gave me directions to her apartment, seven blocks out of my usual territory. I'd never been to an apartment before; all I knew were houses: the box-like, company houses built for Hoover Dam employees during the depression where all my friends and I now lived.

Because I wasn't sure how long it would take me to get to my first lesson, I roller-skated as fast as I could, feeling the vibrations of my metal skates coursing through my body as I whizzed over sidewalks, underneath Chinese elms, across big black streets called Wyoming, California, and Arizona. I climbed the apartment stairs on the toes of my skates, knocked brusquely, then sat down in the hallway to remove my skates.

The door opened, and a pale, thin woman looked out cautiously. "You must be Phyllis Nelson," she said so quietly I could barely hear her. "Come in."

"Yes, that's right," I said, jumping up and brushing past her, full of the energy I'd gathered from the sunshine and spinning wheels.

"You certainly are exuberant," she said, smiling what my father would call an anemic smile. "Leave your skates here." She gestured to a corner by the front door.

I set them down as cautiously as I could, but the skate key dan-

gling from the string around my neck clanked against the wall as
I set them side by side.

"Careful," she said, her hands poised midair as if she were a
Japanese dancing doll. "You might chip the paint with that key."

"Sorry," I said, feeling suddenly bulky and awkward. With care,
I proceeded to the piano stool, set my book bag on the floor noise-
lessly, lifted the blue volume of John Schaum out of the stack, and
opened it to page 24.

"Would you like to play this for me?" she asked.

"UmmmHhhh."

Too naive to be cowed for long, I launched into a zesty version of a Scarlatti sonata. After the first page, she stopped me,
her hand on my elbow. "You don't romp through Scarlatti like
that, Phyllis. And you must observe the rests. The silence is as
important as the sound."

She took the book of Schaum and folded it back until it lay flat
on the music stand. "Now. Start again, only this time, play just
three measures at a time."

She kept stopping me, pointing out the italicized Italian, each
dot, each rest, the *p*'s and the *sf*'s, all the directions left behind by
the composers. And she was death on my hand position. "Keep
your wrist up, like you're holding a rubber ball in your hand.
Higher. Hold it higher."

I repeated the three measures over and over, all the time hating
to be reined in when the whole piece was waiting for me. Repeat, repeat. One, two, three measures until they were pure, no
blurred time values, no cheating on tied notes. I began to wish
for my roller skates to roll me away from this nit-picky business of
three measures. All of life was roaring outside while Mrs. Ramsey
picked away at measures.

Playing for Mrs. Ramsey was like being in a cavernous, cold
cathedral, the kind I'd read about in *Joan of Arc*. Mrs. Ramsey
seemed wrapped in a film of heavy starch. I wanted to stretch over

and touch her thin arms beating out the correct time for me, to feel the human part of the woman sitting there, I knew, with her heart palpitating, her lungs filling and collapsing. Somehow, that felt forbidden.

Finally, she assigned the lesson for the following week, and then surprised me. "May I play for you?" she asked as she stood up.

"Sure," I said, moving off the stool and into her chair as she indicated I should do.

But first, she made a detour. She moved across the living room space like a storybook doll about to pour a storybook cup of afternoon tea, nervously touching the afghans on the sofa cushions and the brooch pinned to her collar. She adjusted the round piano stool to the correct height and sat carefully on the bluebells and roses in the needlepoint cushion. I watched the tight waves in her auburn hair, the deep-set eyes, her long fingers with the subtle rings of gold. Tissue-thin flesh covered her knuckles, almost too thin to keep her bones in place.

She began to play. Her touch was delicate at first, every note clear and precise, but then her fingers became like little machines, humming along, the pistons raising and lowering on the correct keys. The sound was like hearing three pianos played together, so many notes going in different directions, a thundering herd of notes, a factory of sounds.

I waited to hear a lyrical melody which would help me imagine the stories I often heard when I listened to music, stories about lonely goat girls or Peter and the Wolf, but all I could hear were notes—scales going up and down, scales in opposition to each other, chromatic runs, octaves, notes, notes, notes.

When she finished, she turned to me, waiting for me to say something. "You sure can play fast," I managed to say, still overwhelmed by the notes hanging in the air close to my ears.

"Remember," she said, as she handed me my roller skates, "three measures at a time, and someday you'll be able to play as I can."

Even as I roller-skated home carrying my bulky book bag, I tried to escape all the notes still circling my head, but they chased me. I couldn't roller-skate faster than they could move. They were like a swarm of gnats pestering me until I whizzed past my front door and slammed it behind me.

Romance

Dolce   Op. 1, No. 3

Mother bought tickets to the Community Concert Series held at the Las Vegas High School auditorium. She washed my hair, rinsed it in vinegar, and curled it in rags. When it was dry, she unrolled the curls and brushed them to a silky texture.

"A handkerchief for your pocket," she said, handing me a lace square from the newly ironed pile of clothes. It smelled like desert wind and detergent. "And one for my purse. We're off to the big city."

We drove onto the Boulder Highway in our sun-bleached gray car. Fine ladies to the opera. Elegant conversation as the wind blew sagebrush against our speeding car, some of which stuck like bird claws to the grill.

"Oh, dahling," I said to my mother, holding my handkerchief by the pressed corner, waving it in her direction.

"Yes, dahling?" she answered. We laughed.

My shoes weren't patent leather as I'd have wished. They were corrective browns I had to wear for my ankles. "Pronation," they called it at the hole-in-the-wall shoe store where they sold boxcar shoes for nurses and people whose feet rolled to the insides. But they were polished.

A lace handkerchief, mother in lipstick and starch, me by her side, holding her hand as we stood in line to give the usher our tickets, as we walked down the slanting aisle of the auditorium in the soft low light that erased the lines from everyone's faces and soon eased into darkness.

The program said Alec Templeton had been blind since birth. "Tap, tap, tap," we heard before we saw him. He used his white cane to find the piano bench and then turned to us and bowed deeply. A deep, deep bow that felt like a giant sigh telling everyone not to worry, he'd be all right, he could see the keys on the piano with the tips of his fingers and wouldn't stumble and trip. Everyone relaxed into their cushioned chairs for the Bach partita. Clear glass, I thought as he played. Clear like my windows when Mother cleans them with vinegar. Clean before the dust or the rain comes.

"Asturias" by Albéniz was the same—miniscule, millisecond pluckings of guitar strings, except on piano keys by someone who couldn't see what he was doing.

When he came to the Debussy, a magic thread spun out from the piano and wound its way through the audience until it wrapped around my throat and I couldn't swallow. He was bending to touch the keys as though they were the softest skin in the world. I glanced over at my mother whose face lifted in a trance and was slightly wet. His touch was like the gentle wind at my nighttime window that talked through the glass and whispered to come out and play, to ride its curves through the sky, to dip and sail like a hawk. His hands caressed the piano's keyboard as the wind did the corners of my house when it was in a friendly mood. The long vibrating strings breathed, exhaled.

"Please, Mama," I begged after everyone stopped clapping. "I want to meet him."

"Oh, Phyllis," my mother said, the shy Idaho girl suddenly appearing in my mother with the wet cheeks. "Are you sure?"

"He's blind, Mama. He won't notice."

We walked up the stairs to the stage and found him standing among the ropes and curtains and sets and other admirers.

"Lovely to meet you ladies," he said, shaking our hands, one of

ours in each of his. I felt his fingers, their strength, their large-
ness, their bones, their knuckles. My hand stayed in his for a long
time it seemed. I searched its geography. Lovely hand. Warm.

I fell in love then. His eyes were only wrinkles in his face. He
hadn't cared for his complexion somehow—a rough measled look
to it, not like a face, just another part of his body to be kept clean
but not fussed about. His face was an accumulation of defunct
eruptions, unchallenged by poking fingers and acne cream. And
his light-colored hair was thinning. But this was love. His hands.
The way they made music.

He gave me a picture of himself posed with a parakeet on his
finger. The ink on his signature was smudged, but I didn't care. I
carried him home between the leaves of the program, careful not
to bend or crease. I hung him next to my bed with scotch tape.
And I cried sometimes when I thought of the music he played.
The way he touched the piano. And me.

Capriccio

Agitato, ma non troppo   Op. 1, No. 4

When I was twelve years old, I began to feel rumblings inside
that I might exist as a separate entity from my family and that
there was a border to the Eden in which we lived. To confirm
this suspicion, we moved out of the sheltered government town
of Boulder City, Nevada, out of our tidy home on Sixth Street,
and away from Mrs. Ramsey's pyrotechnical piano exhibitions.
We moved twenty-five miles away to another world called Las
Vegas, but barely qualified as residents. Our two-story beige tract
house sat on the last street in town. It faced a wide expanse of
dehydrated sagebrush and drab brown sand that blew more than
it stayed in place.

One day, in this last outpost of Eden, my mother was nursing the new baby and practicing a song from a book I'd never seen before. "When I'm calling you, ooh, ooh, ooh," she sang softly while Kathy suckled. She leaned sideways to study the open text on the sofa. I sat beside her.

"See this book," she said, holding up a red, hardbound book with gold lettering that read *Scribner's Radio Music Library*. "It's one of nine volumes. Look at the bookcase," she said proudly. "Volume seven is grand opera excerpts, volume eight is light opera and ballet, and this book, volume nine, is packed with favorite songs of every character. I ordered them from an advertisement in the Sunday supplement. What do you think?"

"That's a lot of songs," I said.

"Can you play this one?" she asked, as she pointed to the page she'd been studying, "Indian Love Call."

The key signature was in flats, easier for me to read than sharps. "I think so," I said, snuggling into her side before I remembered I was too close to adolescence to be doing such a thing. But my mother was still soft and nice to be next to.

"We're a real team," she said as she put her arm around me. Encouraged by the desert across the street and the fact no one could hear her, she sang boldly and brightly to her audience of dust devils, lizards, me, and Kathy. "Will you answer too, ooh, ooh, ooh." Then she stopped. "Oh! I forgot to tell you. Your new piano teacher will be here tomorrow at four."

"You didn't even tell me you were looking for one." I pulled out from under her arm. "I was supposed to help decide this time."

"But this piano teacher comes to the house, Phyllis, which will make things a lot easier on me. I have this baby now, remember?" She held Kathy up above her head and shook her affectionately from side to side. Then Mother pursed her lips and squeezed her face into that "I love you more than the stars and sky, Baby," kind of look.

"Is she a good teacher?"

"I hope so," Mother said, putting Kathy on her lap and pulling off her plastic pants. "Get me a dry diaper, would you, Phyllis? And maybe you could drop this wet one in the diaper pail?"

Mrs. King appeared the next day in a dust storm. She had curly white cotton hair, four feet eleven inches of height, a sundress which displayed rippling rings of old skin, and, I discovered before the end of the lesson, a penchant for napping. She was a far cry from Mrs. Ramsey, who taught me every exercise known to pianists, always preparing me for the eventuality of playing music the precise way.

Mrs. King insisted on show tunes, fancy arrangements of old standards like "Deep Purple," classics like "Slaughter on Tenth Avenue," and a smattering of boogie-woogie. As much as I felt these pieces were a sacrilege compared with the blind pianist's Albéniz, Bach, and Debussy, they did serve a purpose.

"Phyllis is really sounding good," Aunt Grace said in between stories about her girls on one Sunday afternoon.

"Hot stuff," Uncle Tommy said, two thumbs up.

"Isn't she wonderful?" my mother said as she passed a plate of butter-pecan cookies made for the family gathering.

My father was almost happy to part with his thin supply of money when Mrs. King arrived with Latin American sheet music —"Tico Tico," "Fiesta Mexicana" and "Adios." "Now, you're talking," he'd say, sorting through the bills in his wallet. "I'm glad she's learning to play what people like to hear."

Part of me felt like a show dog with clipped toenails and groomed fur, pampered to make the judges happy. But another part of me wasn't immune to flattery either. I might have been converted to Mrs. King's show business ways, even if she couldn't stay awake or even if she had breath smelling like her intestines had done all the work they were ever going to do, but the memory of the blind pianist kept nagging at me. How could my mother take Mrs. King seriously when there were such vast canyons of difference between Alec Templeton and Mrs. King?

I was in a bathtub boat with Mrs. King, the white-haired gypsy, sailing to a sideshow while carnival music echoed off the porcelain sides of the tub. But my feeling was vague and opaque as I sailed along with the swells of the music and the waves of guilt. I did have a piano teacher, after all. I should be grateful for Mrs. King. I should be grateful for every effort my mother made to teach me music and culture, but somehow, something was wrong.

One autumn afternoon, I heard some information about Mrs. King that nudged me out of my uncertainty. Elaine had heard it from her ex-boyfriend, Alan, who'd been caught in our living room with the smell of beer on his breath. I'd watched Alan back down the front porch stairs while my father issued his decree: "When you can leave alcohol alone, where it belongs, you can visit my daughter." And Mother was right there behind him, bolstering him, a cushion to make the task easier. For some reason, I felt like taking Alan's side, a thing I'd never done before.

"If you tell Mom or Dad I've been talking to Alan, you're dead," Elaine said as she whispered the secret behind the closed bedroom door.

"I cross everything I own, Elaine. My veins, fingers, toes, heart. Everything. I swear." But the secret was taking my breath away. "A beer in one hand. A gypsy." It was pulsing and moving around my insides, searching for an exit, especially when I heard Mother calling me to stir a pan on the stove.

I kept swallowing it back down as I stirred the apple pie filling, but then the beginning of it started to leak out. "I wish I had another piano teacher," I said.

"What's wrong with Mrs. King?" Mother asked as she measured the flour and cut its top off with the flat edge of a knife. "You're lucky even to have a piano teacher, you know."

"She sleeps through my lessons, and she has terrible breath. It's hard to play well if you can't breathe."

"Aren't you being your usual dramatic self?"

"Not really. And—," I hesitated before the next sentence. Despite my best intentions, I relished the anticipation of those words shooting out of my mouth like bombs out of airplanes, dropping on the heads of the righteous and self-assured who sent boys with beer on their breaths to outer darkness.

"I've heard she plays piano at a cowboy bar."

"Who would you be talking to to hear that kind of gossip?" Mother stopped cutting the lard into the flour with the two knives in her hands.

"I can't say, but it's true."

Mother didn't answer right away, so to keep myself from blurting out more information, I concentrated on the way Mrs. King slept at my lessons: she must be dreaming of a tall, virile cowboy moseying up to the piano, tapping his snakeskin toe on the dusty floor, and asking her to dance next to his turquoise belt buckle on her next break. Alan said Mrs. King had been dancing in the Saddle Club with a beer in one hand and her head thrown back like a gypsy. "Why doesn't your mother kick her out?" Alan asked Elaine. "I'm no worse than she is. She likes beer. I like beer."

"Don't say things about people unless you know they're true," Mother said, gently shaping the pie crust into a ball with her hands. "Is that filling ready?"

"Yes, it is," I said, carrying the hot saucepan to a trivet on the cupboard, "and what I said is true. I don't lie."

"But you exaggerate," she said.

I hurried out of the kitchen while my lips were still sealed. I could feel the other half of the secret erupting and ready to spill out—"Elaine told me. I'm not lying."

This deliciously wicked information was tempting me to shock my mother, whom I loved more than my own skin, my mother who lived in a world where everyone who was worth anything abstained from cigarettes, tea, coffee, alcoholic beverages, swearing, fornicating, bearing false witness. She believed in being honest, true, chaste, virtuous in all things. She was a warrior for righ-

teousness, and, for some unknown reason, I all of a sudden wanted
to shock her, make her lose her balance on her white horse gal-
loping toward the unmitigated certainty that the righteous would
rule the world. Something was working tricks on me. It wasn't
like me to use treachery. I was my mother's girl.

As I escaped from the kitchen and ran for my bedroom, I felt for
the first time that my mother was a choice—a flower with white
petals that I could pluck from the center and say "I love you, I
love you not." An uncomfortable gap was widening between me
and the one from whom I could never separate: the woman who
gave me my body and my heartbeat. I felt a pulling, a stretching
away from her. A walking toward the north while she faced south.
A need to turn heel and walk on the path that called to me. I sat
on the edge of my bed, my hands on my knees, and thought of
paths forking, paths going high and then low, paths with rocks,
paths with sand, paths unmarked.

But there was the blatant fact that Mrs. King played piano and
drank beer in a cowboy bar. Therefore, Mrs. King was a bad in-
fluence. Bad breath, her sleeping at lessons, and the fact she was
a C-minus teacher weren't good enough reasons to change my
mother's mind. But beer drinking would.

I curled into a tight ball around my pillow, feeling uncomfort-
ably tainted, as if I were a boar with a large snout who pushed
people without regard. Someone who would get what she wanted,
no matter how she got it. And I felt lopsided.

Nevertheless, that night I found myself in my mother's bathroom, watching her smooth cold cream on her face.

"I don't want any more lessons," I told her as she patted the
cream with her fingers. "I told you I don't like Mrs. King and
you won't believe me. You just want to keep her because she's
convenient. You don't care about me."

"Oh, Phyllis." Mother's eyes behind the slick mask of cream

were too descriptive. I looked away from the hurt I could see. "How can you be so mean when I only want you to keep playing."

"But why do I have to keep playing? These are *my* fingers."

She wiped the cream away with three tissues, put her hands on both sides of her shiny cheeks, and then shook her head from side to side. "You can't stop."

"But what if I know things?"

"Let's go in the living room," she said.

I followed her, both of us in our pastel nightgowns, and she knelt in front of the bookcase. Her finger slid across the spine of each book, and she finally selected the grand opera volume of the *Scribner's Radio Music Library*. "Will you please play this for me before you go to bed?" She opened to page 44 and the "Selected Melodies" from *Aida*. "Once I was in the opera chorus of *Aida* in Idaho Falls," she said.

"You used to sing 'Heavenly Aida' to me when I was little," I said as I slid onto the piano bench. "Don't you remember?"

"I did, didn't I? Funny me." She started to hum as I pressed the first notes of the piece, and then picked up the hem of her flannel nightgown to polish the coffee table for which we'd exchanged twenty-one Green Stamp books at the S & H Redemption Center.

Suddenly, out of my peripheral vision, I caught sight of my mother opening her arms wide, tipping her chin heavenward, and mouthing words as I played the "Triumphal March." I repeated it several times and watched Mother's arms rising higher, spreading more gloriously, until she seemed as if she were Aida herself, the center of the stage.

"Phyllis," she said, her eyes full of Egyptian mystery as she walked toward me, her nightgown billowing from the air blowing out of the heat register. "You can stop your lessons if you promise you'll never stop playing the piano. I'll help you with your chores. You don't have to do any housework if you'll keep playing."

"Never stop playing?" I said. "Never is a long promise to make."

"You play like an angel." She put her hands on my shoulders. "You are an angel. A present from God wrapped in white clouds and silver ribbons."

I reached up and touched my mother's fingers with all of mine, and I felt relieved to feel no division between us anymore, no wicked impulses shaking their cages. Mrs. King was gone. And now, Mother's flesh was my flesh again, our fingers like ladders leading to each other.

"Miracle hands," she said as I felt her soft stomach against my shoulders and the pleasure of her warmth. "I wish my mother could hear my angel at the piano. I wish she were here with us right this very minute."

Elegy

Lento   Op. 1, No. 5

I was the accompanist for the junior high school choir when Mrs. Trombley, the organizer of the Community Concert Series, called me. "Your choir director tells me you can read music exceptionally well. Would you please turn pages for our visiting violinist's accompanist at tomorrow night's concert?"

"The visiting violinist's accompanist?" I asked to be sure.

"Yes, that's right," she said. "Arnold Papp is his name."

I jumped up and down on the kitchen's linoleum to contain my excitement. "Of course," I said calmly into the phone, even as I jumped three more times. Me in the Community Concert Series.

"You might want to wear something dark that night," she said just before she hung up, an incidental phrase not registering as important in the midst of the excitement. "Go to the backstage door on the west side of the auditorium. Look for Arnold about fifteen minutes before the performance."

"Calm down," my father said, chewing the same piece of meat he'd been chewing for several minutes. "And chew your food slowly."

"You'd think you were giving the concert," Steve said.

I slipped my dog Rocky a piece of the overdone pot roast which nobody human could quite break down with their teeth or jaws. He nuzzled next to my hand and wagged his tail, excited for me if no one else was.

Mother drove me to the side door of the auditorium. "You look beautiful, dear." She patted my wrist and squeezed it gently. "I'm sorry I have a meeting. But I know you'll do a good job turning pages."

I walked along the sidewalk bordered by a metal railing to a heavy door painted beige, the only door on the west side of the building. There were no letters or identifying marks to reassure me I was in the right place, but I had no other choice. I pulled the door open with some effort and blinked about twenty times until my eyes adjusted to the backstage arena. Loops of rope hung from the ceiling, three sets of drawn curtains were hanging into the wings, and a high school boy with an angry complexion was running his finger over the lighting panel, hundreds of green, red, and yellow lights, levers, handles, buttons, and strips of adhesive tape with identifying titles written in broad black ink strokes.

Another young man was bending over a folding chair, unlocking a wooden briefcase, and pulling sheets of music out as carefully as if the case were a sanctum sanctorum. Then he tucked them carefully under his arm and turned the key back to the lock position. Stoop-shouldered, his finger to his lips, he stood as if great thoughts were rhapsodizing through his head that was covered with black, wispy-ghost hair.

"Hello," I said with some hesitation. "Are you Arnold?"

He shook his head yes.

"I'm your page turner, Phyllis."

"You should have worn black," he said abruptly, not saying hello, not smiling, not holding out his hand for me to shake. "Nothing should detract from the violinist." He sounded as if I didn't understand.

I smiled at him, knowing he was the one who didn't understand. This was my first time on the Community Concert stage, the same stage where the blind pianist had played. "I don't have a black dress," I told him boldly in the red dress which showed off my olive complexion, Mother had said. "Red is definitely your color," she'd told me as she turned me around to check zippers and hems on the dress she'd sewn for the occasion. She stayed up all night matching notches and battling seams. A rustling red taffeta dress with a velvet bow on the neckline.

"I told Mrs. Trombley to tell you to wear black," the accompanist said. "Black. B-L-A-C-K. Can't you hear?" Then he set his precious sheet music on top of his briefcase, lit a cigarette, blew smoke high into the air, and looked as if the world had been dropped on him soundly. "Okay, okay," he said to himself, holding his forehead in the palm of his hand. "Keep calm, Arnie. You're on the circuit, remember." He interlaced his fingers, worked them in and out, rolled his eyes back, then practiced scales in the air.

"I guess we can't change things at this point," he finally said. "But move as inconspicuously as possible. Please."

When the lights dimmed and we slipped into our place at the side of the stage, he on a tufted-leather stool, I on a folding chair, his words wormed through the tunnels of my mind. I wanted to hide in my arms, shrink into miniature, become an ineffable wisp of wind on the stage.

For a minute or two, the notes on the page raced by me as if they were on their way to the moon: black notes with dots, with bars and phrase markings over their stems, a Milky Way of notes rising past the accompanist who wore long black tails draped over the piano stool. Then the notes seemed to whirl faster, caught in a twister twisting up and off the page. And I had to catch them with my eyes and send them back to their place. "Stay," I commanded as I did to my dog Rocky at the dinner table.

I made my arms stiff at my sides to keep the taffeta still when I stood to turn a page. No rustling sounds allowed. I whispered my body up and down, reached out for the pages as if I were a robot, turned them ever so precisely so the accompanist would have no complaints.

Then I became aware of the audience which seemed far away. They were a blur, gray faces on shadowed bodies, exuding a sense of plague out there in the dark of the auditorium. They were my enemies with cannons ready to blow me away for breaking code, for not wearing black, even if I did a good job and turned every page at the right time. I was dressed in a blaring trumpet of red taffeta on what should have been a pristine stage. The dress was pulsing like devilish neon, and I prayed I'd stop lighting up. This stage wasn't mine. It belonged to the violinist, and I'd tried to steal some of it from him.

There he was, center stage, playing his heart out for southern Nevada. He could have been playing music of a Martian composer, though. He seemed far away. He was a silent film character, bent over his violin, his bow arm moving like wildfire. The accompanist was much more real to me. He perspired, his ghost hair matting in wet strands, his hands pounding furiously at the keys that drowned the sound of the violin.

Mrs. Ramsey's aloof smile came to mind. It was cool like a desert night when all the heat evaporates because there's no foliage to detain it. "No respect for fine detail," the thin lips of my former piano teacher whispered.

After the final applause, I found tall curtains folded in the wings and wrapped myself in them. Out of the yards and yards of velvet, I watched a long line of well-wishers pouring from the audience to kiss the back of the violinist's hand and speak close into his face with puckered "wonderfuls" on their lips. Sequins glittered out from under the edges of mink stoles; diamonds caught light like spoked wheels; perfumes, cigarettes and the carnation boutonniere Arnold had worn in his buttonhole, wafted by my hiding place. Finally, the crowd thinned, and Mrs. Trombley pushed out of the heavy stage door with the violinist on her arm.

"I should say thank you, Miss . . . ," the accompanist said, barely looking my way as he gestured to the violinist that he'd be right along.

"Phyllis," I said.

Not that I expected it exactly, but he didn't say anything else or show any enthusiasm or kiss my cheek and say, "Deserts have more than lizards after all." And I waited, hanging around in the folds of the curtains, waiting for something he didn't know I needed. Or maybe he did know, and didn't want to give it, this something I couldn't put into words.

He straightened his scores and put them in his wooden briefcase. He locked the sanctum with a tiny brass key, said good night to the janitor, and walked out the stage door where I caught a brief glimpse of the violinist reading winter stars with Mrs. Trombley and another fur-clad aficionado.

And I pulled the ropes on the velvet curtain, opening and closing them, watching the way they swayed when they stopped, looking up into the rafters where there were tracks of hardware, an asbestos fire curtain, endlessly looping rope lashed around long booms. I watched the high school student switching off all the lights on the panel. Gradually, everything darkened except the single light bulb that probably always stayed on, a night light of sorts.

I waited for something to happen until the boy left and the janitor told me he had to lock up. I waited while I waited for my mother to arrive in our car. I waited all the way home, while I brushed my teeth with Pepsodent, and when I sighed into the

covers of my bed under the wrinkled eyelids of the photograph—
Alec Templeton, the pianist, with a parakeet on his finger.

Coda

Moderato semplice   Op. 1, No. 6

"I want to study piano again," I told my father one day after he
picked me up from school. I slammed the car door and waited for
the Plymouth to creep out of the warm asphalt clinging to our
tires. I'd done some research, found out the best piano teacher in
Las Vegas—Mr. Slomkowska.

"You've already had seven-and-a-half years of lessons. You told
your mother that was enough, didn't you?"

"I've decided there's more to learn."

"You don't need any more lessons," he said. "I've got all I can
handle right now." I waited until the dishes were done to approach
Mother, the final say in these matters.

"Well," she said, "Mr. Slomkowska probably wants over fifteen
dollars a lesson. We can't pay that much. You know that."

"The music teacher at school says I'm good enough to be better.
It won't be a waste of money."

"But you're already good enough. What are you trying to be?"
She squeezed the water from the dishrag, folded it in quarters,
and draped it over the sink divider. Then she polished the last
crumbs off the cupboard with a swipe of the sponge.

"Better than I am."

"Why?"

"You don't understand."

"If you can't tell me, how am I supposed to know?" She pulled
the ironing board out of the wall and unrolled Elaine's dampened
blouse with the green leaf swirls.

"I'll pay for the lessons myself." I shouted, throwing the wet dishtowel on the cupboard. "Then nobody will have to understand anything."

"Drama again, Phyllis. Spare me."

"This family. . . ."

"We can't possibly understand our temperamental artist, can we?" She mimicked a passionate Hungarian violinist and then returned to the placket on Elaine's blouse. Steam rose into the air.

"I think I was adopted." I leaned against the electric range and put one foot against my knee, stork style.

"You couldn't possibly belong to us, could you?" She darted the iron in and out of the gathers.

"I'll feed Rocky. Where is he anyway?"

"Chasing rabbits, probably."

I went out the kitchen door to the yard with the near skeletons of apricot and peach trees. I praised the wind for a change. It felt cleaner than usual, and its sound covered my ears. I called for Rocky, and he was there, black as the night, wagging his tail, licking my hand and my face.

I crossed my shoes, the right one on top and vice versa, while I waited for Mr. Slomkowska's student to finish his lesson. The piece he was playing in the other room sounded like two gypsies in the night, staring at each other with desire from the windows of their painted wagons. I heard a mumbled conversation, a few crisp octaves played by the teacher, and then watched a slender boy with confused hair appear and push his way out the screen door.

When I turned my head back, there was Mr. Slomkowska looking straight at me. He had a look of Europe in his face and eyes like something I'd seen in *Newsreel* at the movies, something similar to the Sphinx with essential information printed just beneath his skin. He frightened me. I could barely speak.

He showed me into his studio that seemed a dark cave containing the past mysteries of everything. He was surrounded by marble and leather and richly framed oil paintings. His Steinway piano was stacked high with handwritten scores, Kalmus and Schirmer and *Instytut Fryderyka Chopina, Polskie Wydawnictwo Muzyczne*, several editions of the same piece, and a brass lamp. "And where have you studied?" he asked while his eyes narrowed into me like a single headlight beam.

"Mrs. Bourne in Boulder City for four years. Mrs. Ramsey for six months. Mrs. King for three years."

"I'm afraid I don't know any of them." He sat back on his chair, crossed his legs, and dragged his finger slowly across his upper lip. "Who are your favorite composers?"

"Well, I mainly studied in the John Schaum books, got clear through to the G book with the orange cover. I liked the concertos in that book."

"Con-cer-ti," he said, punctuating the air with a finger for each syllable. That finger—strong, firm, unchallengeable. "Play something for me."

Intuitively, I knew I couldn't play "Fiesta Mexicana" or "Malagueña" or "Tico Tico" that my father liked to hear, the show pieces that made Aunt Grace stop talking about her girls, the pieces that made everyone at the ward talent shows rave. Somehow I knew these people in church who loved me and treated me as their prodigy—the best in the West, no question about it—had never met Mr. Slomkowska. They'd never looked into his finely fractionated eyes that had stared down many a score, torn into them, rendered them helpless.

I ran away all the while I played the Chopin waltz for him and ran from his Persian carpets and shelves of books and scores back into the desert sunshine where it didn't matter whether I was cultured or not, where I could laugh and run and not worry about what kind of musician I was. My perspiring fingers slipped off the keys and my knees shook uncontrollably. Every phrase sounded awkward, as if it were a snowman waddling across the ice and falling into freezing water. The pedaling was all wrong, blurring too many notes. The action on his Steinway was much stiffer than my piano. My fingers felt like Siamese twins joined at the sides, great awkward things dabbing at the keys. The lovely phrases, the scales that sounded so good at home, were disjointed and cumbersome. The waltz didn't dance or move or flow. It was dammed up behind the twigs and fallen branches of my mind that kept telling me this was no place for me, no contest I should enter, that Mr. Slomkowska was a great squawking condor who'd scream at me and peck out my eyes for every wrong note or any sign of disrespect for the past.

"You don't need to be so nervous," Mr. Slomkowska said to me, but the wind in my ears was so loud I couldn't hear him. "Play some more for me, please."

"I don't think I want to take lessons," I said while the hurricane blew around my head and body. "But it's so nice to meet you. Everyone speaks highly of you."

"Play another piece, Phyllis," he said, standing up with his hand on a stack of piano scores. "Just go slowly. Take a big breath."

"No," I said, rising higher than the room into the sky where I could fly away from this and flutter my wings and breathe the strong wind of another layer of atmosphere. "This wasn't a good idea. I really do have too much else to do, my church and school activities, to give these lessons the time they'll need. Here's the money for this lesson." I set the twenty-dollar bill on the two black keys next to middle C.

"Why are you in such a hurry to leave?"

I was gone before I was out the door.

My home was comforting, but at the same time disappointing. I was depressed by the bleached blonde coffee table, the clock, the new print on the wall, the wrought-iron plant holder with its curls upon curls of black metal, all obtained from the S & H Green Stamp Redemption Center. Redemption had something to do with Jesus Christ, not stamps pasted in a book, stamps that bought substitutes for the real thing. Where were the Persian rugs and musty volumes of old, well-used books? Everything in my house was new and plastic, and yet everything was so far behind.

Nothing seemed right: my mother wanting music to fill her ears against her mother's words about Aunt Lois's talent; my father wanting audience, laughter, and good times; the violinist's accompanist wanting black when I wore red; me not knowing what to want, trying to please everybody until I was a blown shell of egg, too wispy to stay in any kind of place. My self was falling away from me, lost in everyone's ideas about culture.

It seemed as if music and I were like tumbleweeds, blown every which way across the desert, sometimes clinging to car grills, sometimes soaring with the ravens, sometimes nestling in the corner of a house and huddling tightly against the wall. Who did music belong to? What was it? Where did it come from? Who owned it? Who spoke for it? Mrs. Bourne? Mrs. Ramsey? Mrs. King? Mr. Slomkowska?

My mother wanted me to have it. So did my father. But they only wanted to hear music that evoked memories for them, songs that made them cry or laugh or want to dance. Mrs. Ramsey wanted perfect technique. Mrs. King wanted good times. Mr. Slomkowska—I didn't stay long enough to know what he wanted, but whatever it was, it felt far away, maybe too far away.

I wandered around the house, opening and closing doors to see if anyone might be sleeping. Nobody home. I lifted the top from the cookie jar and found one stale gingersnap that scattered crumbs onto the kitchen floor with every bite. With nothing else to do, I sat down at the piano and looked in the mirror screwed into the top of the piano with flowers-made-of-glass knobs. There was a girl looking at me. A girl with unruly black hair, olive skin, and sad eyes. I tried to smile at her, but she didn't find it convincing.

Without thinking, I found middle C, and my fingers began wandering up the keyboard to take that girl for a Sunday afternoon walk, maybe. As the sound grew higher in pitch, I imagined the sun dancing on the leaves of the trees, speckling the sidewalk, putting a mosaic face on the lawns, the streets, the girl's eyes. And then I remembered the bass register.

With my forearm, I leaned on every low-sounding key I could until a storm threatened our living room. Tons of thunder sheathed in massive gray clouds swept across the ceiling and filled the room. I couldn't hear or see anything else, not the hum of the refrigerator in the kitchen, not the doors, the staircase, or the furniture looming at the periphery of the weather.

My fingers ran up the keyboard to find an umbrella, and as soon as I found it, I opened it with small intervals—seconds, fourths, and fifths—into an octave and a place to protect the girl from the storm. My fingers ran down the keyboard and past middle C to the other side of the street where the girl waited under the umbrella, anticipating the rain that would soon be pouring and running down the gutter in a little stream, then a big stream, and maybe even a river that would cover the street and carry canoes or rowboats or even steamboats past her place at the side of the road.

I played a sailing song with a hint of the sailor's hornpipe I'd learned from Mrs. Bourne and saw the girl hopping from one foot to the other in the narrow space of the curb, and then my fingers strummed a banjo accompaniment while the girl leaned against a light pole and waited for a Mississippi riverboat to go by with cotton bales stacked high on its deck.

Then, it came: the gentle rain. My fingers pressed into the notes that sounded like high sky. Water falling and falling: G-E-C, G-

E-C, sol-mi-do, sol-mi-do, gentle rain, gentle rain. Over and over. Gentle rain, then harsh rain filled the whole street in front of my house with raging water. The storm was getting too big. The girl on the other side of the street might be marooned and have to hunt lizards for survival. So my fingers stopped raining on everything in the city, and the side of my left fist began hopping from a group of two black keys to a group of three as if it were the girl jumping over large puddles. Back and forth. My right hand thumbnail played short glissandos for giant splashes of water.

Fist over fist, my hands climbed the piano and then arched over the keyboard to land the girl in the bass clef and Boulder City again. There she climbed the outside wall of Mrs. Ramsey's apartment and hung from the windowsill to listen to her former teacher playing major and minor scales. She pulled herself up to the window and waved and made clown faces, lips stretched out with two fingers of one hand, tongue zany at the side of her mouth, while Mrs. King played background music sounding like two calliopes playing different songs at the same time.

But the girl needed to return to Las Vegas. I played full piano arpeggios, up and down, until I had a jet car rolling like a fireball back over the Boulder Highway. The girl turned into an acrobat who slid in and out of the car windows and onto the top of the roof where she stood on her hands against the strength of the wind and the speed of the car—Willow Woman with gold-studded bracelets on her arms and her ankles. The car turned corners at 100 miles per hour while she jumped over tree branches and back onto the top of the car. Finally, the car screeched to a halt in front of Mr. Slomkowska's house on Maryland Parkway.

After the girl honked the horn three times, Mr. Slomkowska came to his screen door and squinted against the sun, trying to ascertain what was happening in front of his house. The girl folded into pretzel shapes, a silhouette in the sunlight, a rubber band of a girl who could bend any which way. Mr. Slomkowska clasped his hands together in the middle of his chest, winked and smiled and said, "Bravo. You are an artist. Splendid. *Magnifique!*"

And I played every note on the piano, from the bottom to the top, in chromatic fashion, white keys, black keys, white again, black again, getting louder until I reached the top key. My hands lifted off the keyboard, my arms lifted overhead, my thumbs locked together. I leaned to the right and dove off the piano bench, landing at the bottom of a lake, on the floor, breathless from my journey. I nestled in the shag rug and hugged myself and the girl with sad eyes with both my arms.

I'd been away. I'd seen new places and things. And I rolled over on my back, spread both arms out like a majestic angel would if she had arms, took the deepest breath I could find, and tried to climb back into the music I'd just experienced. I wanted to hold that music in my hand or my head or wherever would hold it for me for just a little while longer.

Thora Jane Mickelsen Nelson,
emergency schoolteacher,
Bonneville County, Idaho, 1944

Herman Evans Nelson,
electrician's mate third class,
U.S. Navy, 1944

Top: Mrs. Mayhew's second grade class, Boulder City Elementary School. Phyllis is fifth from left in front row. *Above, from left:* Stephen, Thora, Kathryn, Herman, Elaine, and Phyllis Nelson, standing.

Sister Wadsworth (*top row, left*), Sister Arnold (*top row, right*), and the

Every Mormon girl's dream: marriage in the temple, especially the Salt Lake temple at the center of Mormondom (Courtesy of the *Deseret News*)

Opposite, top, Learning how to carry oneself like a lady, Bernie Lenz's modeling school graduation, 1960; *bottom,* Learning to respect the laws of the land, Girls' Nation, Washington, D.C., 1960.

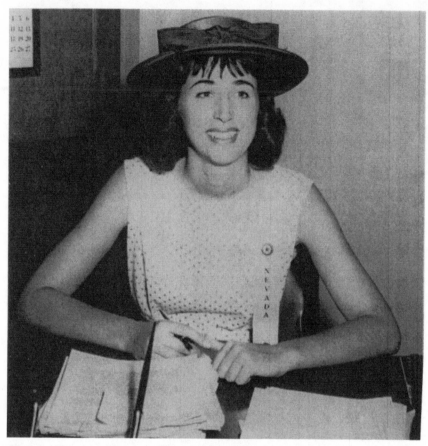
At Girls' Nation, in an assistant deputy's office at the Department of Agriculture

On a roadtrip to Caldwell, Idaho, the real Las Vegas Rhythmettes

Leonard Bernstein receiving a wild west
welcome at the McCarran Airport in Las Vegas

Yes, there are real girls in Las Vegas: the Las Vegas Rhythmettes

Receiving the big diploma from Dr. Walter Long, principal of Las
Vegas High School, 1961

THE RUSSIAN
WINTER
DANCING STUDIO

*J*never did tell my mother the whole truth about Mrs. King, my third and least favorite piano teacher. I never divulged that she fell asleep at my lessons because she drank too much beer or played too much bingo in cowboy bars at the edges of town. Even so, I was definitely surprised when my ex-piano teacher telephoned to ask if I wanted a job.

"How would you like to be an accompanist at a classical dancing studio? The teacher's name is Christina, and she used to dance with the Ballet Russe."

Somehow, I imagined Mrs. King in her spaghetti strap sundresses and tired skin rubbing shoulders with ranch hands in boots and saddles, not someone like Christina who once danced with the Ballet Russe.

I put my hand over the phone. "It's Mrs. King," I told my mother. "She's asking if I'd like to be an accompanist at a classical dance studio?"

My mother's smile spread slowly, as though she were on the receiving end of a generous compliment. "Of course, dear," she said. "You'd love that. You'd have spending money and a chance to keep your fingers agile since you don't have time to practice regularly."

There it was. The old wrinkle, activated. Anything to keep me playing the piano and fulfilling my mother's dream. But she didn't understand my dreams, those wisps and fragments of things foreign. She'd never believe that a classical dancing studio and a woman named Christina intrigued me more than the chance to play the piano.

"When and where?" I asked Mrs. King, and my mother beamed, thinking I was being cooperative.

Mother turned the car onto Ninth Street and stopped across the street from a white stuccoed building with wide panes of glass and yellowed venetian blinds. Gold decal letters on the glass announced that the building was Roberts' School of Dancing.

"Good luck, dear," she said, kissing my cheek.

"Thanks."

When I first opened the door to the studio, half of the room seemed gigantic and half seemed miniature. There was something lopsided about it. At the opposite side of the acre of wooden floor, flanked by floor-to-ceiling mirrors, two tiny women were talking quietly, one dressed in black leotards and the older one wearing a pansy-patterned jersey dress and a small-brimmed black straw hat.

I stopped breathing as I walked what seemed like endless steps toward them. Finally, the one in leotards stepped forward and reached for my hand.

"Hello. I am Christina. This is my mother, Mrs. Sharples."

Mrs. Sharples's smile crumpled into her wrinkled face as she said hello and nice to meet me. She was tiny enough to live in a playhouse.

Christina was taller, but still half my size. She had a body of steel, her hair was tightened in a vise-like bun, and she had a handshake like a wrestler. I slumped to diminish my height and felt like a tarantula from the desert trapped in a glass jar by Mrs. King.

She lead me to a worn upright piano in an alcove, creased the music book so it would stay open, and pressed her hand flat across the top of the pages. "Play," she said.

I wasn't sure if my fingers or brain would function with this intimidating woman standing so closely, but I recognized the simple Chopin prelude on the page. The notes were the same as my music at home. C was still C. D, D. Reliable shapes had followed me like a shadow to this alien place.

But as I played, I felt cold. Christina seemed so brusque, a glacier of self-assuredness, a Russian winter. I wondered if my mother could feel this cold front as she waited outside in our gray blimp Plymouth, and I wondered how this powerful woman had been born out of such a slip of a mother who'd probably topple over in high wind.

"You'll do," she said after I finished. "We'll start in five minutes," and she walked off to talk to the mother of one of the dancers who'd just arrived at the studio.

I ran across what seemed like miles of wooden flooring and across the street to my mother and the Plymouth. "I got the job."

"I knew you would." She shifted into neutral, started the ignition, and blew me a kiss. "I'll pick you up at four, then?"

I wanted to tell her about Christina and how I might freeze if I stayed there, but she gunned the motor and rolled out of her parking place. "Bye, dear," she said.

"You've got lipstick on your teeth," I shouted after her, but she didn't hear me. The car sped to the corner, turned right, and disappeared.

The walk back across the street seemed a gulf. I wasn't ready. But I had no other choice. I entered the front door of the studio once again and put one foot into the wooden arena, the first step of my journey across the barren stretch of floor. Finally I reached the piano, slid onto the bench, and leafed through the pages of *Piano Music for the Ballet Studio*, discovering, with relief, I knew many of the pieces already. At least I'd make it through the first day. Then I sat with my hands folded in my lap and listened to the women seated behind me: wives of hotel presidents, band leaders, and pit bosses; mothers of the dancers warming up at the *barre*.

When the dancing lessons began, Christina snapped her fingers in a strict, even rhythm. The dancers pointed their toes and bent into *pliés* and circled *rond de jambes* with the tips of their slippers on the wooden floor. The mothers sitting in rows of folding chairs watched every movement of their daughters—Antonia, Michelle, Priscilla, Midge, Merry Anne, and Cynthia, their prize racing hounds, their hopes, their spinning children of grace and light. They commented on Michelle's leaps; they counted Antonia's *fouttés* and clapped when she broke her previous record.

As the weeks went by, I noticed Mrs. Sharples was always there in her tiny hat and butter-dish size shoes. Before or after the lessons, she waited patiently while the mothers crowded Christina to make inquiries: "How's Priscilla doing?" "Is Darlene working hard enough?" "Cynthia has the talent, don't you think? If she could only perfect her extension." They leaned into Christina as if they thought closer proximity would improve the prognostication for their offspring.

Mrs. Sharples never said much of anything, just sat on a folding chair, seemingly satisfied to be in the same room with her successful daughter. She always sat beside Mrs. Kranz, the only mother who didn't crowd Christina to ask questions about her daughter.

Most of the time, Mrs. Kranz was bent over handwork of one kind or another—darning, mending, sometimes knitting a sweater—and when she wasn't she seemed to gape, her mouth slightly open to catch the movement around her, especially any movement associated with Merry Anne. Even though she said very little, I think she believed Merry Anne, who was just emerging from her ugly duckling phase, would eventually bypass the other, flashier ballerinas. I could tell by the way she watched Merry Anne. After all, her daughter had the most classical body and the most high-boned cheeks. She seemed sure about Merry Anne and her future as my mother was sure about me and the piano, as Mrs. Sharples seemed sure of Christina, who'd already danced with the Ballet Russe and who now taught young girls in Las Vegas the real art of dancing.

One day, after everyone else had left and their daughters were ready to leave, Mrs. Sharples and Mrs. Kranz stood up to gather their belongings and pull on their coats. I was marking the music book pages with tabs so I could find my place more quickly during the lessons. Suddenly, I felt a hand like a soft dove on my shoulder. "Lovely playing," Mrs. Kranz whispered. "You are an artist." I looked over my shoulder at her, surprised she had spoken to me, and she smiled a barely apparent smile. "It's true," Mrs. Sharples added as she sidestepped past the piano bench, still shorter than I was even though I was sitting down. "Just like my Christina."

And then they were gone—Mrs. Sharples into the dressing room and Mrs. Kranz toward the front door.

I noticed Mrs. Kranz's thinness as she walked to meet Merry Anne and as she unlocked the doors of a bloated Dodge, a cousin to our Plymouth. Then they seemed to sail away, home to Mr. Kranz whom I'd heard made high-quality violins. And I thought about Mrs. Kranz, the quiet one, who seemed confident the world would work the way she imagined as she sat on the back row at the dancing studio.

As the weeks passed, I could play most of the music by rote. Having less need for the printed music, I began to stare at Antonia, the consensus star of the class, dipping her toe shoes in the resin and sweating only slightly as she tucked her buttocks into hollows. With my eyes, I followed her every nuance, twist, and turn, soaring when she did, lifting even higher than she did to the wide expanse of blue Nevada sky outside.

My thoughts must have shown on my face. As Christina handed me fifteen silver dollars pay for the week, me standing tall above her, she said, "You want to dance, Phyllis, don't you?" I blushed. Unprotected by the sanctuary of the piano bench, I was bare while Christina focused her piercing eyes on me. I couldn't answer this woman standing with her arms folded and her foot tapping; I couldn't tell her my dreams of soaring like the sound of a Japanese flute through a forest, of being something beyond the ordinary passage of days.

"Try a lesson," she said, a smile playing at the corners of her mouth.

"I couldn't do that," I stammered. "I'm supposed to play for you."

"I can snap my fingers once a week. I've done it before. Why don't you break out a little?"

With my fifteen silver dollars, I went straight to the store selling dance supplies, bought a leotard and tights, and said I'd be back for the ballet slippers. I flew home and burst in on my mother. "I'm taking dancing lessons."

"You're what?" Her whole wheat bread was baking in the oven, and she was scraping lumps of gluten from the cutting board.

"Dancing lessons. With Christina."

"Why dancing lessons when you don't even have time to practice the piano?" She plucked a steel wool pad out of the cupboard and started rubbing the gashes on the bread board. "You know, I just heard you can get salmonella if you don't take good care of your bread board. You're supposed to sand it down once a month."

"But I want to dance."

"Didn't you tell me you're too tall? You're always talking about feeling like a giant at that studio. And what kind of future does dancing have? Nothing you want. You're throwing away your piano like it's a dead fish."

"I want to dance," I said.

At my first lesson I folded my arms across my body and hunched onto the dance floor, hoping no one would see me. Christina assessed my attire and pulled my leotard up from where I had pulled it down over the tops of my thighs. "Stand up straight," she told me. "Chin up."

She snapped the rhythm, a steady metronome of sound, and I felt as though I stood on the bank of a noisy spring stream, afraid of the flow. I experienced the difficulty of tucking my muscles, keeping my hip down on an arabesque, finding the sheer energy required for a simple *plié*. My legs were shaking after five minutes of *barre* exercises.

But I had one ace in the hole. In my living room at home, I'd rehearsed the *grand jeté* over and over, sometimes knocking the plant stand over and having to repack the soil around the roots. My rehearsals were crowded in our small living room, but now I had the whole floor. I couldn't wait to amaze Christina. If I knew anything, I knew a *grand jeté*.

When it was time for floor exercise, I felt excitement building as I moved to the corner of the studio. For some reason, I looked over and saw Mrs. Kranz leaning forward and stretching tall in her seat, almost as if she had something invested in my performance. Underneath the shyness and the reticence, I think she recognized the fire-breathing dancer disguised in my leotard, the one that wanted to leap out of the perimeters of life as maybe she did. I commenced the *grand jeté*.

Preparation, arms out front, graceful fingertips, toe pointed to

the back, Christina's snapping fingers urging me onward and upward until I felt myself flying through the air, awkwardly at first.
I did another and loosened up. Another until I'd covered the di-
agonal length of the studio.

Christina's usually sober face was slightly amused. "Not bad,"
she said, snapping her fingers for the next dancer. "Keep your
head up next time."

My pulse sped as I lined up at the other corner of the studio to
try a *grand jeté* on the left side, something I hadn't practiced as
much. The second launch was not as successful, but I didn't falter
and kept my head up.

"Not bad," Christina said again.

When I looked at her again, Mrs. Kranz had settled back into
her folding chair and was absent-mindedly thumbing the pages
of a magazine, seemingly staring at nothing in particular. I felt
agitated. I needed her to look up, my quiet ally.

One day when I was at the piano, some show girls from the
Strip walked through the front door—no stage makeup or feath-
ered headdresses. "I long for the Spartan demands of a good
studio," they said from behind large sunglasses as they trailed
their cardigans and oversized bags across the wooden floor.

Just before class, I walked through the dressing room to go
to the bathroom. A show girl stood there, unabashedly naked,
her shorts pooled around her ankles. Another was peeling off her
toreadors and see-through blouse before I could say excuse me
for intruding. I'd been drilled about modesty at the Church of
Jesus Christ of Latter-day Saints, but I couldn't take my eyes off
their bodies sliding into their tights without any underwear. Then
they dashed past me as if no etiquette had been breached, as if
their bodies were everyday things, not sacred temples as I'd been
taught from childhood.

There was pure defiance beneath their stretched Danskins—a different world from canning peaches with my mother, baking bread, and sniffing golden loaves, Brother this and Sister that when we greeted each other at church meetings. A strange wind blew through the windows of my mind and shook the panes etched with the Sunday School words: "Choose the Right when a choice is placed before you."

I don't remember leaving the dressing room, but during the lesson, I watched the two show girls leap across the wooden floor and land with their arms stretched gloriously over their heads. As they danced, they held their shoulders back until their breasts tilted to prominence. Then they laughed boldly and spun like striped tops. I wondered if God would fetter their wings or demand retribution for their brashness, their boldness with their bodies.

I felt a wild bird screeching from the limb of a tree inside myself. It screeched all through an excerpt from *Coppélia*. It made me want to tear my music into confetti, to lean into the piano keys with my elbows and forearms, to climb up on the piano bench and fly over the heads of the dancers through the large front windows that said Roberts' School of Dancing and spread my legs and arms and become like wind that carried birds. My chest hurt as I played excerpts from ballets.

I turned around to see Mrs. Kranz mending, darning some socks slipped over a rubber ball, buried in her handiwork. What was happening behind her small oval eyeglasses? What did Mrs. Kranz think of show girls? Maybe they made her ask questions. Was this what she wanted for Merry Anne? What did she say to Merry Anne when they drove home in their Dodge?—"Don't forget the difference between classical and popular dancing. One is pure."

She dipped the darning needle over and again into the web of thread on the stocking's heel. She was a mother with a thread, a needle, and a sock. Steadily, in and out. Night and day. Caring. Mending. Guarding with curious determination.

A dancer's life isn't for you," my mother said when she watched me move furniture in the living room to clear space. "You can dance at the church dances. You've got your piano, and there's school."

"I'm paying for the lessons myself," I said.

"Enough is enough," she said flatly. "You make me tired, and a cheap show girl is the last thing you want to be."

I hadn't mentioned the show girls who'd come to the studio, so she caught me by surprise. I gathered my defense.

"Why are show girls cheap? I've met some, and they're very nice women."

"Give me a break," my mother said. "You know some show girls, do you? Know about the big world out there, do you?"

"I know a few things."

Even as I spoke, I thought of the bare skin beneath the show girls' leotards and their freedom to do with it as they pleased. Lately at night, I'd been thinking maybe my skin could belong to me and no one else. Why did it have to be God's temple when I lived in it? Why did somebody else make decisions about my body? It was mine, after all.

"It's my life," I raised my voice. "I'll do with it what I want."

"Your life is a part of every other life. Don't think you're a solo."

"I want to dance, and I'm going to!"

My mother shrugged her shoulders as if she were dealing with an idiot and shouldn't waste any more energy on the conversation. But she couldn't resist. "Have you ever seen an old show girl? Marriage and family last forever, but legs, waistlines, and breasts don't, your highness."

"So maybe I don't want marriage and family. It's a moving train with no windows or doors."

My mother sighed. "Young people think they're different, that they can break rules. I'm telling you this to help you, my dear. We're all on that train. Nobody gets off. Don't kid yourself, because you'll make things harder if you do."

"But what's wrong with dancing?"

"Nothing," she said. "We dance here at home."

"But I want to *really* dance. Leap up and fly out the window. That kind of dancing."

"You're dancing any time you move to music, dear."

One day, a once-famous fan dancer came to class for a warm-up. "Do you know that's Sally Rand, the fan dancer?" everyone whispered. I recognized her name, maybe from a marquee or a newspaper ad. Sally Rand. I'd seen pictures of her head and leg sneaking out of a massive bouquet of ostrich feathers.

She was five feet, two inches tall at the most, wore a champagne blonde wig, and had a penguin-like torso, a round, curving stomach protuding out into Christina's studio. Not a dancer's stomach. I wished she'd brought her feathers, but there she was at the *barre*, in profile like a plump preadolescent at her first lesson, her thighs thick, her ankles swollen.

She ignored everyone except Christina, found a stretch of unoccupied *barre*, and closed her eyes to concentrate on technique. She probably ignored us because she knew we were thinking about her age and condition. She must have known about the decline of beauty and the fickle nature of worshipers.

As I played the piano, she closed her eyes to all of us, to her own body, to the veined, wrinkled hand holding onto the *barre*. She bent her knees. She pointed her toe. She lifted her leg as high as she could on the *grand battement* which was only about thigh high. Lifting their legs shoulder high, the young ballerinas outdistanced the stage star. Ignorance being bliss, she kept her eyes closed.

After the *barre* exercises, she excused herself, thanked Christina, then walked to the dressing room not looking at anyone. I saw her neck skin that was beginning to sag in loose hoops. Sally Rand was a mortal who hadn't escaped even if she'd been able to leap once upon a time.

At that exact moment, I knew there were limitations here. I had to find another way off the train.

The lessons weren't the same after that. Half of me wanted to fly through the air, and the other half clung to the ground.

At lessons, the *pliés* seemed harder, more like an exercise in futility because one was so much like another. Maybe the strain, sweat, and muscle manipulation required too much of me. Maybe I was too tall, too busy, maybe I should be practicing the piano. But maybe, I suspected I'd be forever running alongside the wrong train while I could hear the whistle of the right train off in the distance.

My mother says I can't take any more," I told Christina. "Why's that?"

I slumped in the winter of the dancing studio, and folded into myself like a ball of a human being ready to roll away. Folding my arms as if to keep warm, I saw Mrs. Kranz sitting next to Mrs. Sharples, sewing buttons on a sweater, hunched over her work, not looking at me just then.

"But you want to dance," Christina said. "Anybody can see that. What is it that *you* want to do?"

I mumbled. My answer was meaningless, undecipherable, both to me and to Christina. As I looked at the precision of the floorboards, my tongue solid lead, I could see Mrs. Kranz leaning forward, subtly straining to hear an answer.

I felt Christina's hand on my arm—Christina, no longer the Russian woman frozen by eons of winter and ice. She looked up at me, her eyes filled with concern.

"You could be good," she said. "It wouldn't be easy because of your height, but there's something you have. . . . It's the same thing you have in your piano playing."

I couldn't talk. I moved toward the door and the sunshine. My eyes swept Mrs. Sharples in her prim hat who vigilantly and faithfully watched her daughter and never missed a lesson. I looked at Mrs. Kranz's face one last time and thought I saw a look of loss mixed into her expression. Maybe I needed to see this loss because I'd lost something though I couldn't say what it was.

Mrs. Kranz will never know I saw that on her face. I've never seen her or Merry Anne since. She'll never know I've thought of her at times, wondering about her daughter—the most classical of the young ballerinas in Christina's wintry dancing studio, the most aesthetic, the most pure. Where is Merry Anne with the face carved by the heritage of proud cheekbones, too grown-up for her age? Is Merry Anne a show girl? A ballerina? Or is she a computer analyst or a research librarian observing life through small oval glasses? Is she darning socks for her own daughter as she twirls across the wooden floor of a ballet studio somewhere in the world?

And why was Mrs. Kranz so quiet, sitting on the back row absorbed in perpetual mending? A would-be dancer in disguise, like me, even as she posed as a mother?

OMMY AND HERMAN'S FAMOUS STORY: When relatives gathered on Christmas night at our two-story house facing hills of sand instead of drifts of snow, my father and his brother, Tommy, never failed us.

Ritual was the first order of business, however. We had to pray over the food on our buffet table before we scooped and plucked and mathematically figured how to fill a plate to capacity. The children found places to sit cross-legged on the floor, the adults on the sofa or a kitchen chair brought into the living room. Everyone balanced clear-glass hostess plates on their laps, careful not to spill the raspberry punch or topple quivering jello salad and stacks of sliced ham, roast beef, and cheese arranged between halves of Mother's feather-light rolls.

"Herman, you lucky dog," Tommy said. "How did you ever find this woman who could produce such beautiful food!"

"Herman's not a dog," my mother said from across the room, her literal mind offended.

"This food is good," Aunt Grace agreed and pressed her lips together as if she hadn't put enough lipstick on the upper lip and was making last-minute repairs. "That's the one thing Thora sure knows how to do."

Mother looked half pleased, then half hurt. She was constantly wary of Grace's tongue, and at the moment seemed busy interpreting her words. Had she said my mother only knew how to do one thing, nothing else?

"True enough," said Uncle Elwin, whose only entree into Christmas night conversations was to express his appreciation for Mother's cooking. The rest of the time, he stayed tight by his wife Raity's side.

At the back of this small talk was a sense the evening would soon light up. After the dirty plates were collected and Mother's candy was set out in cut-glass dishes, the uncles loosened their belt buckles one notch, and everyone waited for Tommy and Herman to begin.

"Well, you know," Uncle Tommy began, "we weren't always perfect." Everyone laughed, no matter how many times they'd heard him use that line for openers, and everyone settled back in their seats, comforted that the Christmas night story was coming and that things never changed.

Sitting on the floor with my cousins, I leaned against the sofa's seat cushions between Uncle Tommy's and Aunt Grace's legs, also content to know I was about to hear the famous tale of my father and Uncle Tommy almost blowing up the side of a mountain in Ruth, Nevada.

"We'd fallen in with a ring of thieves," Tommy said, "something like Ali Baba. You know that story, don't you?"

"They were the same boys we played with every day, actually," my father, an honest man, said. "I was the smallest one," he continued. "Those big boys lifted me up and pushed me through the window of the munitions shed on the side of the mountain. 'It's in the box with three Xs,' they said as they pushed me into that dark, spider-infested shed. 'Don't throw it out, though, just hand it to us.'

"I fumbled around until my eyes adjusted to the dusky light

and then saw those three big *X*s staring back at me like a poison label on a pharmacy bottle. I pulled the screwdriver out of my back pocket and wedged the lid open. The dynamite looked like cardboard-covered candles with wicks—a thousand of them, it seemed. 'Hurry up,' I heard them whispering like hoarse coyotes.

"I stood on my tiptoes to pass the dynamite over the ledge, then realized I was too short to pull myself up and over the window. 'Get me outta here,' I yelled. They told me to shut up quick, then yanked on my arms and dragged me over that ledge. If I think about it much, I can still feel the pains in my stomach where those splinters scraped my skin."

"And then," Uncle Tommy, the relay runner standing ready with an open mouth, lifted the baton from my father's hand, "we crawled up over rocks, almost losing our footing, almost sliding back down the hill on that loose gravel, but we were like lizards, our bellies scraping over boulders and brambles. Sweat running down our faces, mixing with the dust so close to our noses."

"It was Don Belknap who set the cap and blew the fuse," my father retrieved the telling. "He was the biggest one of all of us, eighteen, which meant he got sent to prison, not reform school. You should have seen the people bust out of those houses below us when they were suddenly besieged with those rolling rocks and clouds of dust."

"Boulders," Tommy said, lifting his arms to recapture the story again. "Gigantic boulders rolling down toward Ruth, gaining speed. I never in my life wanted so much to be an eagle so I could fly to some crevice to hide deep down inside where no one could see me. Boy, were those people mad. One man even ran outside with a gun."

"A gun?" Aunt Grace said, slapping her knees so heartily I felt a breeze on my neck. "That's a new twist. But then, you two have to have at least one new twist every year. Right, Tom?"

Tommy ignored Grace. "Damn rights," he said. "I just never mentioned it before."

"I don't remember that part either." My father folded his arms and looked sideways at Tommy.

"Well," Tommy said, sliding to the front of the sofa cushions, leaning further into the story, not looking at my father, "I do. You must not have noticed it in all the excitement. The sheriff and some men of the town came roaring up that hill like bulls in a fury. They picked us up by the back of the pants and carried us under their arms like we were Christmas hams."

"You're Christmas hams all right," Aunt Grace said, and I turned to watch her throw her brightly painted face back to laugh. I laughed, too, always happy for an opportunity to laugh with the irreverent Aunt Grace who opened forbidden doors. So did my cousins and Uncle Elwin.

"My stomach was still hurting from the window ledge," my father said, interrupting our laughter too soon. "When I got picked up and carried by my belt, I thought I might die right then and there."

"And you should have seen our dad when we arrived home," Tommy said. "Grandpa to you nieces and nephews. He was a picture of the Black Death—black in the face, unbuckling his belt to take us out to the chicken yard where we stacked wood. He must have lashed me with that belt over fifty times. He was one mad José."

"You sure about that?" Grace asked. "Your numbers seem different every year."

"Well, maybe not quite that many." Tommy frowned.

"Maybe two or three?" My father smiled a cat-got-a-mouse smile.

"They were going to send me up," Tommy slid away from any answers, "but Mother pleaded with the judge. She told him she'd make us do dishes for a year and feed those stupid chickens who smothered each other when they got too cold and tried to keep warm. She never let us forget our crime, kept telling us how lucky we were to be at home and not in some wild animal cage with iron bars on the windows."

"They didn't consider me a candidate," my father said, snatching a piece of peanut brittle from the bowl on the coffee table. "Lucky for me, I was too young."

"Well, I was sure in big trouble there for a while," Tommy said. "Lucky Mother had such a convincing way with the law."

For a moment, I thought I heard some unlikely emotion in Tommy's voice, but then, both my father and Tommy grabbed handfuls of Mother's fruitcake, toffee, and peanut brittle. I stretched forward to the same plate and pinched a slab of fruit-cake with the most gumdrops visible—yellow, orange, green, and red all together in the same piece. My lucky night. Everyone else followed suit, and we sat in a momentary lull, listening to the sound of teeth crunching candy.

Sitting quietly between Aunt Grace's and Uncle Tommy's legs, I was wishing we could go back inside the story and that the story would go on and on and never end because when it ended, we were all the same people sitting in the same squared-off, tiny living room with the tall metal gas heater crowding the space. We were something different inside a story; we had possibilities other than the ones in this yellow plastered room. And I wondered if some of the other relatives were wishing the story would end, just for once, with as big a bang as it started.

Every year I kept hoping everyone except Tommy would be quiet. Then the story could really become a story, and something more awful or miraculous could happen to Tommy and my father in Ruth, Nevada, just once. Maybe they'd have to go to reform school where they'd be forced to eat thin gruel for breakfast and dig up old highways with pickaxes. Or maybe a gigantic boulder would be rolling perilously close to a house in Ruth, Nevada, and an angel with wings would appear out of nowhere and lift the boulder into the air in the nick of time.

But even with the same, anticlimactic ending, there was something soothing about the story, maybe because it was always the same with a few minor variations. Maybe everyone was relieved the story wasn't worse and the law had been merciful to two men we loved.

"Wouldn't be Christmas without your candy," Uncle Tommy told my mother when he stood up to pass the caramels to the cousins who couldn't reach the coffee table without social embarrassment. "Wouldn't be Christmas at all."

"Wouldn't be Christmas without your stories," my mother told him as he leaned down to buss her on the cheek.

A SUNDAY SCHOOL STORY: From the time I was very small and my dangling feet couldn't quite reach the bare wooden floor over the edge of the wooden folding chair, I heard at Sunday School about angels, visions, and miraculous healings.

The most important heavenly-being-appearing-out-of-thin-air story was about Joseph Smith, the first prophet of the church. The first version I remember hearing was when I was seven years old. Sister Austin held up three colored pictures of Joseph praying: the first by his bedside, the second in a field while he leaned on a scythe, the third in a grove of tall trees with streaks of white light touching his shoulders and two holy-looking men standing in the air.

"As a very young boy," Sister Austin said as she sat before us with the three pictures balanced on her lap, "Joseph wanted to know which church was the right one to join. He'd studied the King James Bible and read the passage, 'Ask and ye shall receive.' So he asked as he plowed the fields for his father and before he went to bed at night. One day, as he knelt in the Sacred Grove, he was granted a vision. It was a real vision, not just a dream: God the Father, Jesus Christ his Son, and the Holy Ghost actually standing before the kneeling Joseph Smith, bathed in the light of the opened heavens. 'Which is the true church?' Joseph asked them."

"Where's the Holy Ghost?" my friend, Harve, asked.

"I can't see the Ghost either," my other friend, Ricky Traasdahl, said. As a matter of fact, none of the six in our class could find the third party in the Godhead, no matter how carefully we studied the shadows between the rays of holy light in the picture.

Sister Austin chewed on her forefinger for a slight moment. "No one knows much about the Holy Ghost. He's a spirit. An essence."

"Is the Ghost like an angel?" I asked, hoping it might have golden curls and a cherub's face.

"The Holy Ghost is a sacred mystery," Sister Austin said, "but he's not to be confused with ghost stories your older brothers and sisters might tell you. We won't get into that. Let's have a closing prayer now, and ask the Lord to help us understand this mystery in our hearts, if not in our minds. Harve, will you close with prayer?"

He jumped out of his seat, ready to escape the hour-long class.

"Come over by me," she said, pulling him gently by the elbow. Then she folded her arms around him and began speaking the prayer. He repeated it after her, saying the "Amen" rather more loudly than the rest of the petition to God.

The next Sunday, Sister Austin, dressed in a navy blue dress with slanted white lines and a gold chain connecting two buttons sewn on either side of the dress, told us about another heavenly being appearing to Joseph Smith: the Angel Moroni. He was an ancient angel from Book of Mormon times who appeared in Joseph's bedroom in the early 1800s and told him to dig with his father's shovel into the side of the Hill Cumorah in New York State.

"Angel Moroni directed him," Sister Austin told us fervently, fingering the gold chain that hung between her breasts as if it were a magic talisman from fairy tales. Her face was like a slow light bulb working its way up to full wattage. "He struck a stone box, brushed the dirt from the tops and sides, and saw the rusty latch that had been underground for thousands of years ever since Moroni buried it there. Using a lever to lift the rounded top of carved stone, Joseph looked inside and saw not only engraved plates of gold, but the Urim and Thummim—two stones cradled in silver bows fastened to a breastplate. Seerstones for Joseph. Crystal balls. Magic spectacles.

"All of this because he asked God, 'Which one is the true church?' Remember the passage from the Bible we talked about last week? 'Ask and ye shall receive'?" Sister Austin's voice was shaking; she was rubbing the gold chain harder and faster. " 'I beseech thee, oh God,' Joseph begged until God the Father answered him in the Sacred Grove. 'None of them,' God said. 'None of them, except what I'll reveal to you.' "

When she spoke those last words, Sister Austin was swimming in fervor, speaking in a deep spirit voice as if she were God himself. " 'Except what I'll reveal to you,' " she repeated. She sat there blinking, staring out at us, lost in the far-away world of the Sacred Grove where she seemed to be witness to the first vision herself.

We waited like still trees for her to come back to our classroom. Finally, she sat back in her chair, as if spent from her journey to we didn't know where. "Any questions?" she said in her regular voice.

"Would God appear to me if I prayed hard enough?" I asked.

"You can talk to him all you want and he'll answer you," she said, "but no ordinary human can see God—as much as we might wish otherwise. His glory would make you faint dead away on the ground."

"But Joseph Smith was a person like us," I said, noticing the lines on Sister Austin's dress that reminded me of the sunlight slanting on the heavenly beings when they appeared to Joseph Smith. " 'Ask and ye shall receive' are words in the Bible for everyone to read."

"He was chosen," she said. "Ordained by God. 'Many are called, but few are chosen,' the scriptures say. Joseph was a prophet, and we must listen to the voice of our prophets above any other voice we might hear."

I shook my head in agreement even though I wasn't quite sure why.

"Phyllis," she said, stacking her teaching aids in a neat pile on the floor next to her chair, "would you like to say the closing prayer before we go today?" She folded me inside her arms just as she had Harve. She told me the words to say, and I could feel her intensity: "May we always listen to the voice of thy prophets, oh God, and obey thy commands."

As my mother knelt beside my bed that night, I said the regular prayers she taught me, not forgetting to ask for the continued good health of our family and the safety of the missionaries. But just before I said "Amen," I prayed inside my mind where no one could listen. "I want you to come and see me, Heavenly Father and Jesus and the Holy Ghost. I love you as much as Joseph Smith did, honest."

I kissed Mother good night, climbed into bed, folded the sheet top over the blankets, then tucked the covers under my arms. Then I concentrated on the ceiling. Any of the three beings would be fine with me. I watched for a crack to open up, for the tilting moon to pour its light into my room, for the beings to appear in a maze of milky stars.

Just at the brink of sleep, I saw two feet, followed by legs, and a transparent body. I think it was the Holy Ghost because I heard the faintest flutter of wings and the smallest whisper: "I love you, Phyllis. I'll help you find the truth and the way." The being stood beside me, though I don't think he stood on the floor. He leaned over me, so small in my bed, his face the softest outline of gentleness. The light from his eyes and his arms bathed me in waves of love.

As my eyes began to glaze over with a contented sleep, I saw the shimmering outline of a transparent foot exiting through the ceiling. The Holy Ghost had slipped back into the night to listen for other praying children, but he had come to me. He had.

AUNT RAITY'S STORY, ALMOST: Next on the Christmas night program, Aunt Raity took her turn to tell her favorite story—the one about the flatcar. Once on a Christmas Eve, it was pulled by a hissing steam engine into the town of Ruth on frost-covered tracks.

Aunt Raity always looked sad, as if she lived in a bleached seashell with only the echo of the living ocean. Something about her had crawled away and left her to fend for herself. She seemed permanently faded except for the vivid moisture in her hazel eyes when a tender memory was evoked. Even her laughter on Christmas night was often muddied by what sounded like tears in her throat. The relatives said she was just like her mother.

"The flatcar was piled with burlap sacks filled with oranges," she said, patting her husband Elwin on the knee as if his presence made the world a safe place. "Kennecott brought them in for the children of the miners, accountants, truck drivers, secretaries, and foremen who worked for the copper mine. Riding beside these bulging bags of oranges that year was the biggest, fattest, roundest Santa Claus I ever saw. Not like your department store Santas today." She paused to swallow and pull her handkerchief out of her small purse. "He tossed those oranges through the air, and we all caught them. There was a shower of oranges like we were standing under a giant tree dropping everything in its branches on our heads."

"We rarely saw oranges in those days," my father said, his pale blue eyes looking as if they could see the fruit at that very moment. "Catching an orange was almost as good as the silver dollar I got once. Do you have any idea how much a silver dollar could buy in those days?"

"Herman," my mother whispered behind the shield of her hand. "It's Raity's turn."

"And, I'll never forget," Raity said, looking at the ceiling as if it were a movie screen reflecting the past. "That Santa Claus pulled me up to the top of the flatcar. I reached out to him, and he grabbed my hands and pulled me up beside him. He said I was the prettiest little girl he'd ever seen." She dabbed at a sliding tear on her nose. "And he slipped a quarter into my hand and whispered for me not to tell anyone. I never felt richer in my whole life."

Raity's voice broke. The tears came. No one knew what to do or how much attention Raity needed or didn't need at that moment.

"Well," my father said carefully, "do you remember that time I came home with a silver dollar?"

Raity shook her head yes and blew her nose. I watched Mother bump her knee against my father's. "Not now," she whispered.

"Raity won't be able to talk for a few minutes," I heard him whisper back. "Maybe you kids don't know this," he said to the children seated on the floor, "but I used to deliver papers when I was your age." He focused his eyes intently on one particular cousin to avoid his wife, who was still Raity's champion.

"One year I delivered up in Ely's Red Light District." His face turned bright with the words. "The Red Light District," he said confidentially, "is the place where ladies of the night live and conduct their business." He smiled out of one side of his mouth so Mother could see he was aware of the children's sensibilities.

"What are ladies of the night?" a cousin asked.

"Ah," he said, "they were dancers and entertainers who painted their faces, poked feathers in their hair, and dazzled the eye. They were the most generous customers I ever had."

"They're down and out whores," Aunt Grace whispered loudly enough to Tom that I could hear. "Why does Herman always tell this story? Poor Thora. Look at her over there wishing she could change the subject."

I heard the emotion creeping into my father's voice, the emotion so easy to touch, so close to the surface in both Raity and him. I could feel it rising, feelings as much a part of the Nelson heredity as our noses, pale eyes, or bone structure.

"She was probably trying to drum up future business," Uncle Tommy guffawed. "Was she successful?" Tommy winked. The adults laughed, except for my mother. I looked down at Aunt Grace's red-patent shoes with red-patent bows clipped to the toes. Her feet were squirming inside the shoes as if she were preparing another Aunt Grace comment which was usually a cross between a pygmy's poison arrow and a court jester's quips. For once, I hoped she'd keep her own counsel.

"Don't ruin this for me, brother," my father said without looking at Tommy or my mother, or any of us, really.

"Around Christmas, these ladies seemed to know it wasn't too easy being a newspaper boy 365 days of the year in the mud, rain, and snow when you're only eight years old. One of the older women, her name was Francy, drew moles on her cheek and extended her eyebrows with a pencil; she slipped me a silver dollar one snowy day when I was collecting. Do you have any idea how much money that was then? A silver dollar? And she told me I was the nicest newsboy she ever had, stroked my chin with the feather in her hand, and said why didn't I buy a present for my mother and myself, but mostly for myself? She wore a softly woven shawl over a violet satin dress. She had the prettiest eyes. Heavy dark eyebrows. Violet eyes like her dress. Never saw any like them before or since."

My father suddenly looked like a small boy sitting by himself in this crowd of relatives. He was shivering in the icy wind of a high mountain mining town, trying to gather the courage to call out to passersby, "Paper?" The small boy was unnoticed because he was uncertain, not knowing whether or not to apologize for standing there in the cold asking for pennies to take home to his mother.

"Those women were angels," he said, still holding his finger in the air, which meant he had a bit more story to tell. But he paused, unable to overcome the feelings playing havoc with his narrative.

I felt the sympathy rising in me, the quick water in my eyes, for the sense of a powerful gift given my father. I only knew my school teachers, Dr. Jones's nurse, the sisters in the Relief Society. They didn't paint their faces much; they wore simple clothes and no feathers. They helped when a woman in the ward had a new baby or there was death or illness in the family.

Ladies of the night: "whores," Aunt Grace called them; "angels," my father called them. Whoever they were, they seemed to nurture during the hours their sisters rested from the cares of the day. They looked after my father, who'd moved from town to town every year of his life, and sold papers to buy shoes because his father kept stumbling home at night, asking for someone to help him find his bed and the money he'd meant to bring his wife. But those were stories from other occasions, not Christmas night.

"Whenever kindness is present," my father finally said as he wiped his eyelashes with one finger and uttered the last sentence of his story, "God is there, too."

A FROM-THE-PULPIT STORY: I dreaded the two-hour Sacrament Meetings on Sunday afternoons and went well-prepared with a pad of paper, at least three sharpened pencils, and sometimes yarn for a quiet game of cat's cradle. But once in a while, a good speaker came along.

Speeches were assigned by the bishop and given by a church authority, a returned missionary, or an everyday person called out of the congregation who would speak on an assigned topic. The best speakers either started with a joke to relax the audience into a listening mood or by shouting at us to sit up straight and listen to the word of the Lord. We sat up. I'd stop drawing with my pencil and paper, stop whispering to my friend, and listen when those two kinds of speakers stood at the pulpit.

A favorite topic was tithing: whether or not 10 percent should be paid on gross or net; how to find the faith to open up one's checkbook.

The speaker on one particular Sunday had been bred a Southern Baptist and knew how to kindle fire with words. "Do you want to go to the celestial kingdom after you die?" he said so loudly I covered my ears with both hands. Then he pointed his finger right at what I thought was me, right between my eyes, and I knew the Lord was speaking through him. "Pay your tithing."

I'd been weak in my resolve to pay tithing on the money collected in my mason jar at home. I'd considered it lucky money, not earnings to be tithed. I found it under sofa cushions and on the street and by the checkout counter at the grocery store.

"The Lord needs you to get up off your backside and be *for* something, not sit on the fence or be against his principles. If you pay your tithing, you not only pay back the Lord for his blessings, you purchase a parcel of salvation for yourself. Don't cheat the Lord. Don't be selfish."

I examined the hands in my lap, my long-fingered hands that could stretch wider than an octave on the piano, a feat for someone so young. And yet these hands had failed me, failed to put 10 percent of my lucky money in an envelope for the Lord.

"You'll be richer," he shouted. I could see the perspiration popping out above his lip and sparkling on his forehead. "Richer! Do you hear me? You less-than-lions of God think you're giving your money away: 'Good-bye, I'll never see it again, down the rabbit hole,' but your money will come back to you tenfold.

"I heard about a brother who went to the bishop with his tithing on the day he lost his job. He believed, brothers and sisters. He believed. He took part of his last paycheck to the bishop and said, 'I believe in tithing more than I believe in my own earthly survival.' Why, I tell you, brothers and sisters, by morning a neighbor dropped by and said, 'Here's two bushels of wheat. My crops have been mighty generous. And by the way, could you possibly lend a hand? I'd gladly pay you.'

"This neighbor didn't know the man had lost his job, I swear on this pulpit. He just had an urge to share his blessings. But you know what this urge was, brothers and sisters, don't you? Yes, you know! It was the Holy Spirit. The Lord who wouldn't let one of his faithful servants down, not then, not now, not ever! And I exhort you children to ask your mother or father for ten pennies in change if you only have a dime in your piggy bank, and then save one of those pennies for God. I promise you in the name of the Lord who reigns above us all, tithing is a divine principle that will bless your lives, not take from them. I say these things in God's name, Amen."

His collar was wet now, and so was I. Under the arms. Underneath the hair at the back of my neck. But underneath the wetness, I'd been kindled. I was burning for God as I raced home on foot, unable to wait for my parents. I ran to the mason pint jar wrapped in a towel in my underwear drawer. I poured my pennies onto the bedspread and counted out what was there and divided it by ten, feeling glorious all the time to be obeying God's principles.

When Aunt Grace and Uncle Tommy came over for dinner, I showed them my envelope filled with tithing, signed, sealed, and ready for delivery to the ward clerk.

"Fire insurance," Aunt Grace said. "The Mormons think they can buy fire insurance for the apocalypse."

"Not now, Grace," Tom said, looking over at my mother, smiling at her, easing her past any offense she might take from this irreverent talk about her religion.

"You won't ever let me have my say," she talked back. "Just because Herman and Thora and their kids believe, it doesn't mean the rest of us have to." Then she laughed, much to Tom's relief. "There are two things I'm not supposed to discuss here," she said. "And one of them is politics. Right?"

Tom couldn't win. She was always one step ahead.

"Thora," she said, "maybe you have a story to tell? It's the only safe thing we know how to do together. Tell us about the time your brother was killed by lightning."

AL JOLSON SAVES THE DAY STORY: "Just how many schools did you attend?" Aunt Grace asked my father as she passed him the caramels my mother had boiled to soft-ball stage, cooled, and wrapped in plastic. "I never can get that straight because it seems like you Nelsons were forever moving around."

When Aunt Grace wasn't talking about her daughters, she was subtly scratching the paint on the Nelson family image. She always did it with charm, adept at hiding her frustration with her in-laws and her husband, Tom. She both loved and loathed this man she couldn't shape into the right mold, the same one who happened to be a part of this Nelson clan, no proud clan as far as Grace could tell.

"Well, I think," my father said, "let me see. One, two, three . . . maybe eight elementary schools and five high schools."

"No wonder you Nelsons are such a crazy bunch," Aunt Grace said, charming most of the children with her laughter, her smile, the things she could get away with.

"Dad believed the next bend in the road was the perfect place to stop," Aunt Raity said with charity in her voice. She was sitting even closer to Uncle Elwin, her hand laced into his even though he seemed to be counting the minutes until he could say good-night gracefully.

"We saw a lot of living," Tom said, leaning back on the legs of the kitchen chair, patting his stomach with both hands. "We met lots of people from San Diego to Salt Lake City to Brigham City, Utah, where we returned four different times; then there was Nevada—Ely and Ruth, and then Idaho."

"We lived in a warehouse once." Raity looked up at the ceiling again, and I saw Elwin squeezing her hand and patting her wrist.

"Just for a short time," my father defended as he sat up straight in his chair. "In Ely. We were waiting for a company house to become available."

"We always had lots of friends," Tom said. "Hundreds of friends everywhere we moved. And our family was close. We loved each other. Poor little Mother had a hard time of it, but she loved us more than her own skin. We'd do anything for each other, I swear we would. And we always had a good time laughing, making up jokes, playing pranks on each other. Anybody want some gum?" he asked, pulling the tab on the package and taking a piece for himself. "I brought a giant pack tonight for anyone who wants some. You pass it around, Steve," he told my brother, "and everyone give him your wrappers so Aunt Thora won't have a big mess to clean up."

"Remember Mary Jane?" Raity's eyes brightened for the first time that evening while the package of gum made the rounds. "The way she'd go out in the streets and do impromptu music theater on the sidewalks? Remember how she sang 'Swanee' better than Al Jolson? Remember how she'd tap dance through a crowd of miners until one of them handed her a nickel or a dime? She never asked for money, but they gave it to her. Mary. I wish she were here now. Little Mary. Why won't she come spend Christmas with us?"

Sometimes I thought Raity's tears waited just under her eyelids, waiting only for the next tender moment to show themselves. I never ceased to be fascinated by her eyes—pale, hazel, almost faded as if the sun had stolen the color from them. Raity's eyes were full of some unnameable sorrow, some regret that could never be satisfied, some hole in the middle of her somewhere.

My father and Raity had inherited their mother's eyes. I'd seen pictures of Grandma. Pale, pale eyes. Too much flooding, too many tears. Tommy's eyes weren't pale, though. They were snapping brown, swarthy, desert eyes like his father's. He seemed tougher than Herman or Raity. Maybe his eyes made him stronger and more vital.

"Will somebody sing 'Swanee?' " Aunt Raity asked. "Does anybody know it? Phyllis, can you play it on the piano?"

I shrugged my shoulders. None of my piano teachers had taught me "Swanee," although all of us children except for Kathy could sing, "Swanee, Swanee, *how* I love you, *how* I love you," in the Al Jolson way, emphasizing the "how," shaking our palms every time we sang it. Our father taught us that much one evening after we finished dinner and he had no appointments to keep.

"My dad can sing 'Swanee,' " I said, curling one strand of hair on my finger mischievously.

"Yeah, Herman," everyone clapped. "Let's hear it from Herman," Tom shouted, chewing his fresh piece of Wrigley's rapidly on one side of his mouth.

My father didn't need much encouragement. He and Tom could be talked into performing any place, any time. "A family disease," Aunt Grace called it. "You'd think they were good or something."

My father sank to his knees and walked on them to the middle of the room. "I hate to make Al Jolson look bad," he said, "but all idols have clay feet. Right?" Then he clasped his hands in the middle of his chest and put pleading into his arms and face. "Swa-nee. Swa-nee," he talked rather than sang, changing his clasped hands from one side to the other, convincing his audience he loved dear old Swanee. "*How* I love you, *how* I love you. . . ."

I looked up at Aunt Raity, mouthing the words with my father, her face shining with wetness. Then she covered her mouth with her handkerchief and placed her other hand over her neck to disguise the sobs pulsing against her throat and chest.

Then Tom stood up and fanned his hands out wide. "If only

I had those white gloves Jolson wore," he said. Then the two brothers sang the words, "My dear old Swa-nee," together. All the children jumped up from their places on the floor and mashed into the two uncles, jumping, hopping, skipping, singing, "Swa-nee, Swa-nee," until everything got rowdy and one of the cousins knocked over a chair, and my mother said, "Oh no, you've put a hole in the plaster," and everybody began talking all at once until it seemed as if it was time to go.

UNDER THE QUILT STORIES: My mother was the star quilter, master of the tiny stitch. Everyone asked Thora Nelson to help when they wanted a beautifully quilted quilt.

Until I was six years old, I went with her to the houses where quilts were finished, and I played underneath the fabric stretched to the clamps at the four corners of the frame—a cotton backing, batting, and a pieced top. Playing with chipped building blocks or drawing with dulled pieces of crayon while needles darted in and out of the quilt top, I sometimes stared at the designs of my mother's leg hair mashed by the nylons she rolled down to her calves. Sometimes I tied and untied her broad-heeled black shoes with the saltshaker holes punched in the toes. I compared her legs with the other women's, their rolled nylons, their thighs spreading flat on their chairs, their sturdy black shoes. But most of all I listened to the talk.

I heard the sisters wince when they pricked their fingers with a needle and the next minute complain they could never find a needle. I heard them talk about new babies, recipes, and the family who was to receive this quilt.

"It's too bad about Brother Beacon losing an arm in the gravel crusher and sinking into such an abject depression. His wife is such a light, and she's had nothing but trouble. Thank goodness she's got faith like the Rock of Gibraltar."

"She's had a hard life, hasn't she? She's always been such a pretty thing, but that hasn't helped her much. Did you ever hear her talk about the time she saw one of the Three Nephites?"

I stopped untying my mother's shoe to listen more carefully. A woman in a rose-colored dress was talking. I couldn't see the top of her, only her lap, her sensible shoes, her hand underneath the quilt, and her pointer finger capped with a thimble.

"Don't pass this on, but about two years before she married George, she was accosted by a stranger when she was out in the desert looking for arrowheads. Her sister told me about this, though she didn't exactly tell me the whole story. I think the man molested her and left her in a heap. She tried to find her way home, but was confused and probably couldn't see anything but her shame. She'd walk one way, then another, and all the time it kept getting darker.

"But she was clearheaded enough to get down on her knees and pray to the Lord. And right after her prayers, she stood up right next to the shoulders of a man in a white suit who pointed his finger in a westerly direction. 'Follow this creek bed,' he said. When she looked down and saw the dried gully, she knew it hadn't been there before. And she swore to her sister she'd been looking for just such a pathway back to town.

"When she looked up to say thank you, the man was gone, nowhere in sight. Disappeared. Poof. I'm just sure it was a Nephite."

"You don't hear those stories as much as you used to," someone else said. "The one I heard when I was a little girl was when Brother Whitmore, my grandfather's friend, stopped over at a house in Kanab, Utah. He'd arrived late and had to leave early, so he left his horses hitched.

"He was tireder than a dog's ear after being in the wind, so he didn't respond immediately when he heard the Spirit whispering to him in the night. 'Go and move your wagon,' the voice told him. He rolled over. 'Go and move your wagon,' the voice insisted. He turned onto his other side. 'This is your last warning. Move your wagon, now.'

"Brother Whitmore finally realized he was being spoken to by that still, small voice we've all heard about. He pulled on his boots and went outside in the chill of night to move his wagon and horses to the other side of the house. Immediately after he pulled his covers back over himself, a bolt of lightning zipped out of the sky and struck the cottonwood tree arching over the house. That big old tree split in half and fell right smack in the spot where the wagon had been. I'll never forget my grandpa telling me that story, and you can bet your bottom dollar I listen when that still, small voice whispers to me."

"Me too," I heard several women saying together.

"There's got to be spirit life all around us, don't you think? The departed know everything we're doing. That's why we'd best behave ourselves."

"Definitely. Why, I think when my husband died, he stayed around to attend his own funeral. I could feel him there, just like he was sitting next to me, dressed in his Sunday suit and straightening the knot in his tie."

"Sometimes I think my little boy who died is watching over me," my mother said and my ears opened wider than before. I'd only heard stories of how he'd died in her lap on the way to the doctor's, how he took his last breath; she said she'd never forget the sound of the death rattle.

"Sometimes," she continued, "I think God assigns members of our family to watch over us and guide us through difficult times. I was with Sister Rasmussen when she was ready to die, and she said when she reached her hand out, she felt someone clasping it. The veil is very thin, don't you think? All that spirit life out there? All those angels watching over us?"

And I looked at the canopy over my head: the quilt and the quilters' hands. And I imagined beyond that canopy, beyond the ceiling, beyond the roof of this house. I saw a crowd of women quilting in the sky, talking about us, telling stories about our sins and misgivings. They shook their heads and puckered their lips

in prayer that we'd all remain faithful to the end and see beyond
our mortality into the wide skies of God. Maybe there was a big
hand reaching out to me if only I could reach far enough with my
faith to catch the little finger. That hand was poking through the
veil into the real world, reaching out to me like my mother's hand
was reaching underneath the quilt to pat me on the head and say,
"It's time to go now, Phyllis."

THE KING OF STORIES: The doorbell rang. Everyone
was surprised because the Christmas night party at Herman and
Thora's was almost over. The clock said nine-thirty. Consensus
had been growing that it was time for everyone to be getting home
and let the curtain drop on Christmas for yet another year.

When the doorbell rang, my father opened the door, and the
king of stories came into the living room like a prince, a duke, a
man of royal blood: my grandfather in a rare appearance.

He hadn't brought his new wife, Helen. She'd been waiting a
long time for him, pursuing Grandpa when Grandma was still
in place. Helen was convinced Grandpa needed her and only
her, and she'd finally captured him. But Raity, Herman, and
Tommy weren't ready to forget the woman who'd mothered them,
changed their diapers, taught them to tie shoes. They wanted
Christmas to resurrect their mother's laughter, even if it had been
bittersweet. They wanted the memory of their mother's eyes even
if they had to look at Raity's eyes to be reminded—those uncertain windows unable to hide her hesitation or her apology for
taking up space on earth.

So Grandpa came alone.

"We were wrapping things up," my father said, "but there's still
some of Thora's candy left."

"Just as well," Grandpa said. "I can't stay for long. I left Helen
by herself."

He was a little man, squat in some ways, not in others. Sometimes he seemed imperious, as if he'd been crowned king once upon a time. At other times he seemed to be running after the crown that had rolled off his head one day. Without his crown, he was a commoner. But even though he never found it, he didn't shed his courtly ways or forget he was king of stories. He could shine the inside of a story into pure gold.

"Always a story," my mother said in disgust because of the way Grandpa didn't pay much mind to his wife, who was sick with melancholia, the way he'd stay out late at night drinking, telling stories to people too drunk to care. "Always a story," about where he'd been and what he'd been doing when he explained to his wife at 2:00 A.M. One story built upon another, a house of stories upon stories, floor after floor, stacks of stories, and who could ever tell where the truth was in all that flurry of stories?

Aunt Raity and Uncle Elwin scooted over from their places on the sofa. "Sit here, Dad," Raity said, patting the cushion. "How's my little daddy?" She squeezed his bicep as he sat down and then rested her head on his shoulder for a brief second.

"Fine as things will allow," he said, straightening the knees of his trousers, but then he was back up again, center floor. "Children," he said. "Do you want me to tell you about the time I was selling eggs and had to balance my way across a railroad trestle? Or do you want me to tell you about my favorite chicken who fell down the outhouse hole and squawked like a mighty condor until. . . ."

"What about the one about the cow that showed up out of nowhere?" my mother said.

"Well, all right," Grandpa said. "If you insist." He cleared his throat and held up his hands as if he were preparing to conduct his audience. Then he closed his eyes for a minute to concentrate before he began with words.

All of us children were looking up at the man standing in the middle of the floor on the beige sculptured carpet. He seemed to have a glow on him, almost as if emanating from a portable spotlight he carried with him for occasions such as this. He was a man who'd seen the world and lived to tell about it; he was a mystery man we'd heard about in whispers—a man who bought a new car when he hadn't paid for the one he had, a man who had enemies because they owed him money, a man who came home late at night and made our grandmother cry. We'd heard the whispers.

"He acts like he's been drinking again," Grace whispered to Tommy as she tapped her right foot close to my knee. They forgot me sitting at their feet, privy to their clandestine commentary. "He never shows up on Christmas night. What's he doing here now?"

"Shhh," Tommy said. "He's ready."

Grandpa stood in the middle of our living room as if he were a treasure to be revered and appreciated, a wild turkey spreading its tail, a man alive because he had an audience to validate him, saying, "Yes, yes, you are the king." Still looking for his crown.

"As you children know," he began, his eyes still closed, "we never had much money when I was a little boy. There were eleven of us, not counting Mom and Dad."

"You sure you don't want to sit down, Fon?" my mother asked.

"No, no. I like to stand when I tell stories." His eyes were opening. "My mother was a real stickler for the church, you know. She followed every admonition given her by the authorities, one of them being tithing. My dad wasn't quite so attached to the principle, but he could see how upset she was when he told her they'd better not pay their tithing this one particular month. They didn't have it to pay.

"Well, as you might imagine, Mother went into a tailspin, crying like a reed pipe in the wind, wailing how the Lord would take care of them if only they had enough faith. Where was his faith? She was going to take their last money to the bishop then and there. Right that minute.

"My father could see she had her mind made up, so he said he'd walk with her over to the bishop's. They had nothing to lose, he guessed, except they wouldn't be able to feed their children now. He hadn't done well by them, he confessed as they walked.

"When they handed the bishop an envelope with the last of their money in it, they didn't say it was all they had. They paid as if this was the smallest pittance possible in their vast fortune raining down from heaven above. The bishop smiled and said, 'The windows of heaven shall open onto you. The sun will shine so bright you'll wish you had a windowshade to pull down. Bless you, my faithful brother and sister.' "

"Wasn't that just before his dad did himself in?" Grace whispered more quietly than I'd ever heard anyone whisper and still hear it.

Grandpa pulled at his jaw, stopped to think about something, his mind stretching further out of the room than before. Raity's eyes were moist, as well as my father's. My mother looked at all the children, pleased we were all tuned in, rapt witnesses to this finer moment of our grandfather.

"Well, for two days we didn't have anything to eat. Mother was afraid to borrow from the neighbor again, so we chewed on the last of the wheat we'd stored in the basement. Chewed it like chewing gum. Speaking of gum, Tom, why do you chew it the way you do? It doesn't become you."

Tommy was startled. I could feel his body react because I was leaning against the side of his leg. "Sorry, Dad." He pulled the gum out of his mouth and wrapped it in a corner of scratch paper he had in his shirt pocket.

"Just about the time our stomachs were gnawing like rats in an empty loft, this brown and white cow wanders up to our door. I mean up to our door, not into the yard. She walks up and talks to us with a long moo. No rope was hanging on her. She didn't look like any of the neighbors' cows. She was new to our eyes. We'd never seen her in anyone's pasture. And she was ready to milk. Full and tight, her teats spread out like swollen fingers.

" 'Whose cow is that?' my mother asked.

" 'Nobody's I know of,' my father said. 'Fon, you run around to all the neighbors in this part and ask if any of them are missing a cow.'

"Well, I ran as fast as wind around the neighborhood, then ran back to the house with the good news. And nobody came looking for that cow, either. Not one person. That cow was probably brought to our door by one of the Three Nephites. Led right to our door by the Lord's anointed."

He held his hand in the air with his last word. No one spoke while his hand stayed in the air, the fingers pointing upward in praise of God. He held us as if we were an orchestra whose strings he didn't want to stop vibrating. Then he closed his hand and thumped his heart once with his fist.

"And with that," he said after a slight pause, "I must go back home. I wish you all a happy new year. I wish you all faith. I wish you all peace. May one of the Nephites help you if you're in need and the angels smile upon you."

I hated the end of his story. He knew how to weave the words and his hands and his eyes together into the magic requisite for a tale. His story was the only one being told on earth while he told it. His was the last word.

Everyone broke into clusters, shaking hands, kissing cheeks, wishing "Merry Christmas" one last time before it was too late. I watched my mother put her arm around Grandpa. "Thank you for that beautiful story, Fon. You touch my heart every time you tell it. Thank you, and please tell Helen we missed her."

"Hypocrites," I heard Grace whispering as she gathered her

skirt to stand up and while her red-patent shoes squeaked. I still sat on the floor with my back resting on the sofa's seat cushions. "Both Thora and your dad. Can you believe she can say she missed Helen or that he can tell a story like that and not tell the whole story. Then he walks out of here and lives the way he does."

"Be quiet, Grace," Tommy said. "Have a little respect for the man."

"Respect! Him?"

"He's my father."

"But he's so full of bull, even you say so."

"He's my father."

And Grandpa walked the full circle of relatives, saying goodnight to his children, then looking each of us grandchildren straight in the eyes and telling us to have faith like his mother had faith, then we'd be able to find the way.

"The windows of heaven will open for you," he said to me as he held my hand in his, not letting me act on the impulse to escape. "Everything will be given to you; all will be understood. You are a good girl, aren't you Phyllis? Obedient to God's and your parents' word, aren't you?"

I shook my head yes, trying not to show the shame I was feeling in this act of supposed affection between a grandfather everyone whispered about behind his back and his granddaughter who heard all the whispers. The words of his story, the whisperings I heard, Grace's words, all were liquid in my head. What manner of man was standing before me? Whose hand did I hold? Which stories were the true stories? Could I kneel and ask God which?

Standing outside the stories, I could feel them colliding with each other. They tumbled from everyone's mouth and filled my ears until I was confused by them. But every time I was inside a story, there was no confusion, only the clarity of a tale spun and the sound of the spinning wheel.

So as I held my grandfather's hand, the only thing I could

think to say was, "Will you come back sometime and tell us another story?"

"You like my stories?" he said.

"I do."

It was Christmas. All was calm, all was bright. The cardboard story of peace on earth was arranged on top of our Baldwin spinet—an awed Joseph, a round yon Virgin kneeling over the glow of her heavenly child. I'd felt the same sense of love when the Holy Ghost slipped through my ceiling not so many years ago.

Filled with this serenity, I smiled at my grandfather. I held his hand until we became another story, he and I. He was the king of stories, and now I was the queen at his side. My grandfather could be anything I wanted him to be. He was safe with his hand in mine.

MAMA PIRANHA
AND HER INSTINCT
FOR RHYTHM

*W*hen *you wish upon a star, makes no difference who you are.* I once believed that line and believed every wish I made would come true. I could ask God. I could ask the stars. Someone or something would answer. But I never took the notion of rhythm into account.

I thought I knew what it was in 1956. My family and I gathered in front of a television set one Sunday night to eat popcorn and watch a performance of a select group of Las Vegas High School girls on Ed Sullivan's variety stage in New York City. The Las Vegas Rhythmettes, the precision marching dance team with their pseudo can-can routine and full line pivots, danced and kicked and snapped their page-boy-hairstyled heads that glistened like shampoo ads.

The camera panned in on each face.

"That's Brother Crane's daughter," my father's voice sounded surprised. "I wonder how he feels about his daughter dancing on the Sabbath."

"I imagine he's ashamed," my mother said, wiping a spill from the coffee table with the corner of her apron. "His daughter parading herself around in that skimpy outfit."

"There's Melba Simmons's best friend," my sister Elaine said. "She's really stuck on herself."

"This is stupid." Mother retrieved the empty popcorn bowl. "Making such a big deal over these girls. I know dancing when I see it. That's not dancing."

But I was mesmerized by the eighteen girls who marched into our home and the full-screen, black-and-white portraits of each of them filling the TV. I would have given anything to be making rhythm with them. I imagined my face on TV, smiling out on the nation, listening to disembodied voices saying, "My, isn't that a beautiful young girl? She could be a star."

At bedtime, the ritual began: "Dear God. I don't ask much, but please, if it's okay with you, let me be worthy." And then, for insurance, I whispered to the sky, "Star light, star bright." I'd take any help I could get.

After I fell into sleep, the black-and-white television images followed me to my dreams and split in halves—legs dancing on the bottom left of the screen, arms synchronized on the upper right side. Marching feet pranced; girls' heads snapped to the right, then to the left on every eighth count; absolute precision, the line of eighteen girls with their hair turned under gently at the tops of their shoulders.

Suddenly, the leg of one of the Rhythmettes snapped off on a high kick and flew through the air. Kicking at the darkness, it landed on a stage swept clean by desert wind. There it danced by itself, until gradually other parts fell into place—an arm, the other leg, a torso—until it was me, Phyllis Nelson, all together, kicking and dancing in the spotlight of the moon on a hill in the middle of the desert, dancing for the snakes, lizards, and cactus blossoms while they stopped and watched. The night sang.

When I entered Las Vegas High School the next year, I watched the Rhythmettes in the girls' locker room slip in and out of the

sleeves of their Rhythmette sweaters. I watched them walk gracefully around the school with their long flowing hair and mani-
cured fingernails. I watched them dance at the halftimes of the
football and basketball games. And I often paused at the bulletin
board in Miss Stuckey's office in the gym. She'd tacked up rows
of pictures of *her girls* marching in parades and shaking hands
with Frank Sinatra.

"That's all you think about, isn't it?" my mother said after I
mentioned tryouts were coming up. We were shelling peas for
dinner. "You think you're really going to be something if you're
a Rhythmette, don't you? It's ridiculous, everybody clamoring to
get into that corny organization, making so much out of nothing.
Set your sights higher, Phyllis."

"I pray to God and wish on stars, Mom. How high do I have
to get?"

She almost laughed, but was too intent on dissuading me.
"What about your music? What about things that really matter?"

"I'm reading the Book of Mormon, and I go to church three
times a week and seminary every morning at six forty-five, even
though the teacher has sawdust for brains."

"Watch your mouth, Phyllis," she said sharply as she ripped the
string from a pod and funneled a handful of peas into a quart jar.

"Why does everything have to be the way you want it?"

"Young people are so blind." She washed her hands with a
worn bar of Ivory, a long discolored brown crack in the soap. She
wiped the water from her wedding rings with a stained dishtowel.
"Deep in your heart you know what's important. You know your
purpose on this earth."

"Oh, and what's that?"

"Letting your light shine, Phyllis. The light of Christ who is
the light of the world. Jesus didn't need to be a Rhythmette to be
loved. Neither do you. The real joy in this life is in God's plan
—being a mother and multiplying and replenishing the earth.

Not in some trumped-up organization like the Las Vegas Rhythmettes. It's phony."

On a hot April night, 127 girls and I filtered onto the shining gymnasium wood, tiptoeing around the edges of the sacred
black and red Las Vegas Wildcat painted mid-floor. The wooden
bleachers were pushed against the walls. Everything shone—our
scrubbed faces, our hair, our eyes, the bright overhead lights.
Some of the girls came in groups of two or three friends, some
with their parents who lingered at the heavy green doors and
watched wistfully while their daughters signed their lives over to
Miss Stuckey.

One paper we were asked to sign asked for our consent for up
to twelve hours a week and up to twenty-five when rehearsing for
the show of shows—the Rhythmette Review. Another was a ques-
tionnaire on why we wanted to be a Rhythmette, what the word
meant to us, how dedicated we thought we could be.

"Being a Rhythmette means I can be a representative of Las
Vegas High School," I wrote. "I can learn discipline; I can learn
how to work with a group of young people my own age in a con-
structive manner."

The paperwork completed, Miss Evelyn Stuckey told us to sit
on the floor. Cross-legged or on one hip, everyone sat tall enough
to be noticed in their coordinated outfits, bermuda shorts, striped
blouses, ponytails, frizzed bangs, curled eyelashes, plucked eyebrows. Every girl, I supposed, saw at the back of her mind an
image of herself full-faced on the Ed Sullivan Show, the center
of the screen. Or had an idea of herself following the footsteps of
the Rhythmette once chosen runner-up to Miss U.S.A.

I, too, scented the major leagues, a chance to jump the never-
stopping train I was on where the rolling wheels repeated mile
after mile: "Obey God's word, obey God's word." More important
than anything—obey God's word. I and 127 other girls sat on the

gymnasium floor, sniffing the scent of opportunity and wanting a piece of it. How could I not step on this golden rung, follow these urgings toward the big times—dressed in a formal evening gown and being introduced "MISS PHYLLIS NELSON" at the Rhythmette Review, the most glamorous show in all of Nevada outside the hotels and casinos? ("Wholesome glamour," Miss Stuckey claimed in an interview in the *Las Vegas Review Journal*.)

I looked at the black painted lines marking the basketball court boundaries and sensed there were no boundaries for me if I could only be a Rhythmette. Then I noticed the gymnast's horse shoved against the wall of the gym. If only it would come alive and gallop to me in a show of favoritism. I'd jump on its back, race across the gymnasium floor, and rein to a stop by Miss Stuckey. "Madam," I'd say. "Ultra rhythm, at your service."

"If you're chosen to be a Baby R," Miss Stuckey was saying, looking over the tops of her reading glasses at every face in the group while every heart skipped two beats, "we expect your best. If you can't give it, don't stay a minute longer." She had angelically curly hair and a charming southern drawl which barely covered the iron will we'd seen snatches of during PE. "Anybody want to leave?" Not a stir on the floor, not anybody shifting position or tying shoes, nothing. Over the easygoing collar of her wool plaid shirt, her eyes swept our faces with one more hawk-like gaze.

"All right. Then I understand each of you is willing to give your A-1, all-time best effort to the Rhythmette organization?"

We all nodded solemnly.

"The senior Rhythmettes will supervise this tryout," Miss Stuckey added, "though all my girls will teach you the routines. I wish every one of you could make it, but, sad to say, there are only six places in the line, plus one alternate. One hundred plus just doesn't fit into that number." Her laugh was something out of the slow South, a high chicken sort of claim on the barnyard. "If you don't make this cut, come to me and I'll tell you what might help you next year. Let's get rolling."

I wish I'd been more aware as I listened to Miss Stuckey that night. There was a Big Wheel rolling across the gymnasium floor of the Las Vegas High School gym with its immaculately shining floors, overhead lights glaring like hospital operation room lamps onto the wood's waxed surface, the smell of April and watered lawns and warm nights. A Big Wheel, a Plan, a Purpose. Round turnings, rollings, me a miniscule part of the tide, rolling along, singing a song, thinking I could bust out by becoming a Rhythmette. I wish I'd known how to listen to the quiet, offbeat side of me that didn't need to prove itself or make a major statement. But I could only hear the public side of myself, so indiscriminate, a sucker fish snapping at the bait, a marionette jumping at every chance to be on stage, the part of me insistent on forcing the bloom.

As I sat there, trying to concentrate, the moon shone through the high smoky windows in the gym and said, *Hey, Phyllis. What are you doing in that tight little box of a gym?*

Moon, I answered. *This is important.*

And why don't you wish on me instead of the stars?

Nobody wishes on the moon, I whispered.

Why not? the moon's lips crumpled. *I'm more like you than the stars are. They gradually burn to death, while I only change my faces and pull the tides.*

What do you mean?

You'll find out. Meanwhile, don't waste your time in that gym. You've got big rhythm, like me. We're sisters.

Joyce Ahern introduced herself. "I'll be your teacher tonight, but first I've got to tell you that Rhythmettes is one of the greatest things that could ever happen to you. It's really fabulous if you make it."

There were eight of us in her group. Joyce was nothing short of a porcelain beauty, white skin and upright eyelashes curled to perfection by the cage of an eyelash curler. Could my thin nose and what felt like chicken-bone arms ever translate into something like Joyce, her black hair turned gently under at her shoulders? How could I ever get my stick-straight hair to curve like that?

The music started. "Tequila," by the Champs, a routine the Rhythmettes had performed at the state basketball championship, their best ever. Afterward, everyone in the bleachers stomped their feet and jumped in the air yelling, "Tequila! Tequila!" in a wild, mad frenzy of school spirit.

"Roll your arms," Joyce said, "like in a mambo." We learned the part that went with the arms—rolling back on one heel while stepping on the other foot. Then we clapped our hands, put them on our hips, and jump kicked.

I had the grades to qualify, the dedication, and I learned quickly, so I made it through the first and second cuts. But on the following Thursday when it came time for the final judging, the braces on my teeth caught the entire spray of light from the overhead lamps, and I knew the four judges sitting in a tight clump on the bleachers would be blinded to the real Phyllis Nelson, the girl who believed in answers to prayers and wishes on stars. My skin felt like a tight nylon stocking over my real dancing self, and my lips quivered.

When I heard the needle drop into place on the record and the sound of scratchy space before the Champs started strumming their guitars, my body started acting up, working against my will, and slipping out of control. I forgot part of the routine; I crossed my legs when I should have kicked them, and I didn't sink into the beat of the music.

I've always wondered what happened that night. Maybe my body was in league with my mother despite my intentions to the contrary. Or it may have wanted to stretch out under the moon on the desert sand when everything was velvet and still, when the tarantulas and horseflies were asleep, wherever they slept. It may have preferred the black night, a reprieve from the pressure of my mother standing in a window framed by sunlight, shaking her finger at me, always reminding me I had a purpose to fulfill, a rhythm I couldn't escape even amidst cold wars, communists, Sputniks, stories about Bugsy Siegel and the Mafia drilling holes in his skull, pictures of the show girls in the *Review Journal*, relaxing on chaise lounges by swimming pools, their derrieres rounded like rising suns, and more pictures of such things as Miss America, Miss Nevada, Junior Miss Nevada, Missy Nevada, or even the Rhythmettes.

I finally worked up the courage to go to Miss Stuckey's office in the locker room and ask her why I hadn't made it. She reached for a clipboard bulging with paper and leafed through the pages.

"Phyllis Nelson, hmmm." She kept leafing. "Here it is. They've marked the box that says your sense of timing needs work. But you did quite well otherwise." She looked up at me and eyed me as if I were a new product at the grocery store. "You just might have a chance next year if you can work on your rhythm somehow. See what you can do."

I was so excited I wanted to leapfrog over the locker room benches. Rhythm was the problem, not shyness, awkwardness, or my undeveloped body. I could fix that in no time. I could already keep four beats to the measure when I played the piano, I danced the rumba with my father sometimes, and I could feel that rhythm beating inside me. I knew I had it. My rebel body was to blame the night of tryouts, making me get out of step just slightly.

"Dear God," I beseeched again as I knelt by my bed to pray that night. "If you'll help me with my rhythm, I promise I'll always and forever obey the Word of Wisdom. No tea, coffee, cigarettes, beer. I'll be chaste, too, a pure vessel for thee, dear Lord." Then, as I snuggled into the mattress, I vowed to discipline my knees and thighs and arms so absolutely that there'd be no mistake next year.

First, I tried the high school dances. After standing on the side-

lines on too many Friday nights, however, I knew I'd never get
in enough dancing to control my rhythm. Luckily, Uncle Tommy
came by the house one night and mentioned the church dances
held every Saturday night at the Stake Center.

"Sometimes my combo plays at those dances. You oughta come
out some time, Phyllis. Give me a little high sign when you do."

I'd heard about the Stake dances, which were open to teenagers
of all nine wards in the Las Vegas Stake. They were announced
every Tuesday at MIA—the Mutual Improvement Association for
clear-eyed Mormon youth, the place where we heard endless
lessons on chastity, obedience, and purity. But I hadn't considered attending until Uncle Tommy said he'd be there, playing his
trumpet for the Saints' teenagers.

In my mind, those dances were a comedown—a place for the
backwater people, not the movers and shakers. There was nothing
challenging there—no high school football players bunched on
the sidelines telling forbidden jokes or brooding James Deans to
frighten me into speechlessness. There were only shy, awkward
Mormon boys, not unlike me, a shy, gawky girl with eyeglasses
and massively full lips I tried to hide by drawing better, slimmer
lips with my lipstick brush.

I felt bigger than the gray brick Stake Center on Eighth and
Linden that first Saturday night. As I peeked inside, I saw the
walls of the church building's recreation hall were lined with ancient folding chairs, the crowd sparse and unremarkable, and the
four spotlights in each corner of the room amateurishly placed.
The people looked like pale cardboard figures posed along the
wall. There was no jungle here, no danger of being eaten alive,
but there was no sign of any raw animal power either. I walked
into that recreation hall almost as if I owned it. I breathed easily
and didn't perspire as I did on Friday nights at the high school
where I was terrified to dance, terrified not to.

If only I'd been less cocky, looked more carefully, or watched for the signs: the chaperones' hands on my back pushing me gently through the doors, their eyes beckoning to the waiting row of boys, their ears listening for blood racing like a dragster through my veins in the face of my unfolding purpose on earth.

Uncle Tommy was there with his combo. He pulled the microphone to his lips like a sweetheart. "This dance is dedicated to my niece, Phyllis Nelson, and all her little friends. Stand up, Phyllis."

Burning red sped from my toes to my cheeks as everyone looked my way, and I hoped nobody knew I'd come all by myself and didn't have any little friends to speak of to protect me from this glaring moment. Then, quite unexpectedly, I felt blue/violet/green peacock feathers spread over my head as I became the momentary center of interest. I bowed my head and backed toward my folding chair to hide my shame and my pride. When I became a Rhythmette, things like this wouldn't happen.

"Phyllis. Come on out here," Uncle Tommy said, his amplified voice big in the hall. "We'll play a nice danceable little tune, and you choose the first partner for a Snowball. A one and a two." His hand started jumping with the rhythm of "Night Train."

My big chance, here in this pond with pale fish, here in the same building where General Authorities traveled from Salt Lake City to speak to the gathered nine wards of the Las Vegas Stake four times a year and told us to be in the world but not of the world, to scorn pride, never to put ourselves before God.

The boys seemed to cluster more tightly in their groups as I walked toward them in search of a partner. As I moved closer, I felt a surge of power in my chest, me getting to approach the boys, to touch one of them on the shoulder and say, "I choose you," without having to hope and wring my hands and wait for them to come my way. The only unprotected boy I could see was about five inches shorter than I was.

"Would you dance with me?"

He rolled his eyes backward. "Out there? Just you and me?"

"Come on, you two," Uncle Tommy said into the microphone. "Let's get things going. Just a few steps on the dance floor, then you can both choose other partners. Ni-i-i-i-ght Train," he sang. "Ta daa da daa da daa da daa da-a-a-a-a."

The short boy stood there like stone. "No way," he said.

The music was loud—the night train chugging away from me. Everyone's eyes were watching the drama, even though they pretended to be talking. Suddenly, I grabbed his arm. I pulled him. His planted feet slid across the wooden floor until we reached the middle. Then I took his unwilling hands in mine. He was too surprised to run, and he couldn't have anyway, caught as he was in my strong piano hands. We circled and circled until Uncle Tommy's voice cut through. "Choose another partner! Hurry up. Chop chop."

I didn't want to let go of this boy's hands or let him run back to the safety of the wall since it meant I'd have to ask someone else. But the need to be in command of rhythm rose up in me. I'd repeat what I had to repeat, do what I had to do.

I asked the next boy with a fresh callous on my heart. Who cared if he liked me or not? Or, for that matter, if I liked him? The people at the Saturday night dance didn't count anyway.

I didn't miss one dance the rest of the night. I'd ask a boy before he had a chance to move toward anyone else. If there was the slightest chance no one was coming my way when a new dance began, I was out drumming up business, too restless to wait. My intended sometimes escaped to the boys' room, but there was always another in his place. Short, pudgy, or sullen. I was in charge, or thought I was.

As I look back, I realize I was like a scavenger feeding on unsuspecting fish, using those awkward boys who were groping, as I was, for a place in the schema. They were used by Mama Piranha and her instinct for rhythm, the driving force in her life. They weren't companions; they were nutrition for the Rising Star who would eventually leap out of the murky waters and into the sky where stars shone next to the moon. But then I, too, was nutrition—for some bigger piranha, swimming alongside, a little behind and to the back of my line of sight.

My sense of singular triumph at the Stake dance faltered as soon as I stood under the speckled-dome sky and saw the moon. My father and his Mercury drove me home to East St. Louis Avenue and the stark mirror in my yellow upstairs bathroom. When I saw my stringy hair and oily nose, I quickly turned off the light and the truth of the reflection staring back so wolfishly. Then I turned on the hall light, a twenty-five-watt glow, to illuminate me more charitably while the soft light of night poured in through the open bathroom window. No harsh electricity above the medicine cabinet. All I could see were the broad details of my face, none of the fine or not-so-fine particulars of my pimples, braces, and the oil always beading in the crevices of my nose. "When you wish upon a star, makes no difference—"

Before I fell into my bed, I raised the venetian blinds and gazed at the window full of trumpeting moon and blaring stars, still egging me on to make wishes. But my usual Rhythmette wish seemed a pale pinpoint next to this shocking sky which piped music to my ears so much grander than "Tequila" or even Mozart and Beethoven.

My memory is filled with odd shapes of fish swimming across the black of night. Big fish. Little fish. Piranhas and whales. Fish circling the earth, circling past my window on East St. Louis in Las Vegas, Nevada. Fish with wings that began to flap and rise above the watery sky until they were passing through the moon and their eyes became stars. And everything was water and sky and oceans of air and my house began to rise to the top of the ocean until it floated past the moon like Noah's ark.

Hi, Moon, I said, shouting from my bedroom window.

Hello, Phyllis, the moon said. *What do you want to wish tonight?*

I want to dance. And sing and make music. Let me have my moment, Moon.

Your mother doesn't think it's a good idea, and I like your mother. If only she understood that what you want is just a substitute for the real thing. Actually, you're right on schedule.

The moon didn't understand being on television, hearing cheers after my heels at the basketball games, circling the floor and waltzing like a princess at Rhythmette Review time. The moon was so big and already had its place in the sky.

I don't have to listen to my mother and you about everything.

The moon laughed until the whole sky and its fish-wispy clouds shivered. *It seems*, the moon said, *as though you want to be a star for people to see, not a star for people to see by?*

Who are you to talk? I want to glow on my own. And for always, not just sometimes.

I don't always shine, but don't be fooled. That's the beauty.

April. Sophomore year. Now or never. I knew I had to steel my way through this, not allow my body to rebel on me—my knees to shake, my nose to shine. With my babysitting money, I bought a glue-like deodorant to block all perspiration. I applied waterproof mascara and eyeliner to make my eyes large and cat-like with techniques I'd learned from my friend Ronnie Freed. I minimized my lips with a dark line drawn on by a new lipstick brush that clicked when the bristles came out and clicked when they went back inside. When the moon tried to talk to me and make me lose my concentration, I covered my ears with my hands.

And I kept my mother at bay. At the tryouts, I was like a Roto-tiller breaking up the soil, a disturbing machine determined to be noticed, determined to be a Las Vegas Rhythmette. Nothing else mattered.

In addition to the Saturday night dances, I'd stretched my legs into the splits all year to equip me with the highest kick, done

100 sit-ups a night for a flat stomach, repeated exercises to increase my bra size. I chanted "I must, I must" while I pressed the heels of my hands together and pumped. And I watched for any idiosyncratic disruptions of solid rhythm. My heart was calcified.

On the day the new Rhythmettes were to be announced, I stood tightly packed in the middle of the twenty finalists who waited behind the locker-room door, listening to the castanets of "Lady of Spain" while the senior Rhythmettes did their last routine for the student body of Las Vegas High School. When the applause ended, the seniors lined up in a row at the opposite end of the gym. A thin black microphone stand had been set in place.

The finalists were hidden behind the locker room's slightly open door. Some were clinging to Saint Christopher medals, some were checking their hair in the mirrors, some were mumbling silent prayers. But everyone was secretly anticipating the sound of her name sailing across the empty gym floor, floating over the heads of all the students crammed into the bleachers, her name spoken into the microphone loudly enough for everyone in Las Vegas High School to hear, a name to be reckoned with and remembered.

The announcements started from the short end of the Rhythmette line. The shortest senior walked toward the microphone. She was handed an envelope. She opened it. She read it. She spoke the name. Cheryl Henry screamed and almost tore off the door's hinges getting out to the gymnasium where the green-painted bleachers were filled to capacity. Through the crack in the door that had been pulled closed again, I watched Cheryl run across the gym floor, her arms wide open until she slammed into the arms of the senior Rhythmette who'd called her name. They hugged and jumped like mayflies.

The next senior stepped out of her place in the line and up to the microphone.

I can't remember what happened then because the sound of

the next name was so alien to the sound of mine. "Nancy Atkinson!" My ears went numb, Arctic, and the whole room seemed a blizzard, with me huddling in animal skins, waiting for the cutter to break through the ice, throw a rope, and lift me. But I heard something through the storm's howling. Names being called. My name being called. Hands pushing me through the crowd.

"Phyllis, you made it."

I don't remember the trip across the gymnasium floor. I don't remember if people cheered or just clapped politely. After all, there were people out there who hadn't made the finals, people whose girlfriends hadn't made the finals, and here was I, Phyllis Nelson, a dark horse, walking, stumbling, running. I'd won. I'd controlled the elements, despite all the nattering from the moon.

I was slotted into place at the tall end of the line, and the music began. Squeezed between two other girls, shoulder to shoulder, I started across the floor. But a tiny moment of claustrophobia flashed through my head, so small I only remember it now. It had to do with eighteen dancing dolls and their choreography—always using the left foot to begin, turning their heads every eight counts, holding their shoulders back, tucking in their stomachs, smiling, always smiling as instructed by Miss Stuckey.

Crushed into my place in line and thinking in sets of four and measures of eight, I felt shut in for a brief second. What had I purchased? Another train ticket? For one small second I felt myself marching away from real rhythm where dancers threw themselves against the shadows of fire while the earth and the moon beat the drums. Real people howling at the moon, shaking their fists at the wind and the rain.

The new and the old Rhythmettes marched across the wooden floor. The line of girls was not the straight arrow line for which the Rhythmettes were famous, however. It rippled like water. We were Baby Rs, on our way to being grown-up and bounteous and leggy and ready for the grown-up world where our prancing legs would someday spread apart to make babies and birth babies or avoid babies or wonder why we couldn't have babies, all in accordance with the plan. We were being danced on our way by our hormones, by the mandate for procreation, by the rhythm of life, not knowing it was bigger than we were.

Dancing fools, me first among them, kicking headlong into our purpose on earth—to multiply and replenish. Miss Stuckey doing her part by preparing us with manners and stage presence, but really preparing us as gifts for the men who watched, men subject to their own hormones as we strutted and paraded across the stage, displaying our wares for them, the particular curve of our hips, the winning smiles.

The claustrophobia passed, however. I was one of the girls. A Las Vegas Rhythmette. I was somebody, and the football players and James Deans would have to reckon with me. No more Saturday night dances. I counted now.

The bright colors of the moment caught my attention, and I exalted in the fact that I, Phyllis Nelson, had arrived. God bless America. And the stars and the moon. Even my seminary teacher. It didn't matter when I overheard someone in the crowd filtering out of the gym saying, "How did Phyllis Nelson make it? She's so skinny. She walks like a primate."

And it didn't matter when my mother pretended to congratulate me. Her "Good for you, Phyllis," sounded hollow, echoing all the arguments we'd ever had about the importance of not getting sidetracked from God's work of being a lighted candle, virtuous, lovely, and of good report.

On that day in that time of my life, I could overlook all slights and forgive and bless everybody. I had arrived. I could dance up the stairway to the stars, clapping my hands and turning in synch with all the other women who were ever girls. I didn't know my mother didn't need to worry. I wasn't privy to what the moon already knew. There's no escaping rhythm.

LENNY AND
THE RHYTHMETTE

J watched the New York Philharmonic as they gathered on the makeshift platform. Some of the musicians looked as if they could use a transfusion. They'd probably been out all night gambling and who knows what else. After all, they were in Las Vegas.

Even though I was disillusioned from my encounter with Lenny the night before, I was excited for his baton to start the music that was supposed to be purer than anything I'd ever heard. I sat with the Young Friends of the Symphony in the balcony tier of the convention center's round auditorium dressed in white gloves and a black velvet frock. We sat behind the orchestra, face to face with Leonard Bernstein, rubbernecking to get a good look at this God of the East and All Things Musical.

"Lenny's such a man," Mrs. Dickinson had told us the week before at the Young Friends of the Symphony meeting held in her living room. "He's such a lion," she added, almost growling as she spoke. She was the choral director at Las Vegas High School and the driving force behind the Young Friends.

"We've pulled off the greatest coup this side of the Mississippi!" She was backlit by an oriental lamp with a gathered fabric shade and was almost dancing in front of us thirty some high school students recruited from the marching band, orchestra, and choir at Las Vegas High School. We'd been promised an A for the term if we joined up. Not a bad deal, especially if we'd be cleansed of our cultural impurities as the choir director, Mrs. Dickinson, said we would.

The conductor, who had walked past me like a specter the night before, lifted his baton higher, but neither the noise nor the light in the convention hall was dying out. People were pointing, laughing, and turning every which way in their folding chairs. I imagined the audience had imprisoned the New York Philharmonic and herded them into the center of this Roman coliseum to play for their lives. For a minute, they seemed bigger lions than Lenny, waiting to devour him and the orchestra. They were dressed in everything from net shawls and red tuxedoes to bell-bottoms with fringe sewn down the sides, bolo ties, leather vests, a few cowboy hats, peacock feathers poked in stiffly sprayed bouffants.

I had a good view of the tense muscles in his cheeks, the raptor eyes glowering as the raised baton failed to hush the unruly crowd. None of the woodwind players, string players, or percussionists were moving a muscle, totally attentive to their leader, but the audience wasn't following suit.

He lifted the baton even higher, trying to stand taller in his shiny patent-leather shoes, trying to subdue Las Vegas, if not with the tapered baton, then with the force of his imperial self.

The Young Friends of the Symphony had been trained when and when not to clap; we'd been taught to say "Bravo" if we especially liked the performance (though we all said "Brave-O" at the meeting to scare Mrs. Dickinson). We were all trying hard to sit at attention on the turquoise-colored cushions, our hands folded in our velvety laps, our attention riveted on the conductor. I was trying not to feel superior to those who didn't know symphony etiquette or to the technicians who'd left the overhead lights shining brilliantly on the conductor and his orchestra. This was the basketball crowd, after all.

Impatiently, Lenny's arms fell to his sides. He motioned to a man sitting on the front row dressed in a powder blue tuxedo who hustled to the stage pronto. The man's pleasant smile turned into panic as he listened to Bernstein's words. Then he hurried for the door. Lenny paced the stage like a caged animal until finally, the balcony lights dimmed. But those on the main floor did not.

As I watched like a spying angel from the balcony, a technician in a seaweed green jumpsuit moseyed up to the stage, mañana style. Lenny knelt at the platform's edge and pointed to the ceiling. The technician shook his head no, no way, you're out of luck, buddy. Then I watched The Lion turn on the technician, who seemed to grow smaller and smaller as the blast from the conductor melted his contours.

From her place on the front row, Mrs. Dickinson appeared between them, flapping her hands as if they were tiny wings. The technician backed away. The conductor dropped his fists to the sides of his cutaway jacket.

Meanwhile, the man in the powder blue tuxedo had climbed the stairs onto the platform, picked up the length of cord leading to the microphone, and was speaking into the public address system, "One, two. One, two. Testing," and an electronic scream pierced our ears.

After calming the storm, Mrs. Dickinson climbed the wobbly stairs carefully in her rhinestone-covered shoes, radiant in her strapless emerald green gown with a basket of black netting around the shoulders.

"Ladies and gentlemen," she said into the cavernously echoing microphone. "Ladies and gentlemen, please. Technical difficulties aside, we have some of the best musicians in the world here tonight who need to be treated with respect." She wagged her finger at the audience. "Let's show them Las Vegas knows its p's and q's." She patted the conductor sympathetically on the back and returned to her seat, and an uneasy quiet spread over the audience.

The first five minutes went well. The pastoral gamboling in Beethoven's Sixth settled the audience, and I closed my eyes to visions of woolly sheep grazing on uneven hills. But then, I became aware of small agitations beginning as if they were clothes in a washing machine window. Ring-covered fingers reaching, earrings sparkling, bow ties twitching, people leaning to whisper, a baby bouncing on its mother's knee, Brownie attachments flashing. A woman in the orchestra seats who hadn't removed her lynx coat or tinted glasses sent her maid through a pair of double doors. The maid wore a starched ruffle bobby-pinned to her hair and a short black dress which stopped short of her knobby knees. A few minutes later, she returned with a tray of popcorn and cellophane-covered Cokes in red cups. A small trickling of thirsty people followed suit, and the lights on the main floor showed everyone in high relief, every cough, every yawn, every pair of jaws chewing gum, every nodding head.

I pretended to be appalled by all this. I said "shhh" and sent death wishes loud enough for other Young Friends to hear. "They should be so ashamed," I whispered. But inside I was not totally sorry the conductor and the New York Philharmonic seemed to be drowning in the Vegas Valley Sea between the peaks of Sunrise and Mount Charleston.

A week before the concert, I heard Mrs. Dickinson talking to Miss Stuckey, in the Rhythmette office.

"Could you send at least ten of your girls," Mrs. Dickinson was asking, "to greet the maestro when he arrives this Sunday, eight thirty P.M., special charter, Trans World Airlines?"

Miss Stuckey had often received similar requests. Even Ed

Sullivan telephoned her when he heard about Las Vegas's wholesome honor students and real live girls, who actually danced together in the windblown valley.

"I need ten Rhythmettes to go to McCarran and greet Leonard Bernstein's airplane on Sunday night," Miss Stuckey announced at our Monday morning rehearsal. The early morning light reflected on the sheen of the waxed gymnasium floor, setting the stage for the shadows that would play on the wood throughout the day. Some of the high windows were effervescing with the glare of the rising sun. Miss Stuckey shaded her eyes.

"Who's Leonard Bernstein?" one of the junior girls asked.

"The director of a famous orchestra," Miss Stuckey said.

"He's really handsome," I said, having seen his picture in the Sunday paper and having heard Mrs. Dickinson describe his silvering hair, his fierce eyes, the way he *was* music, the fire, the soul, the passion of music. I imagined myself walking down the airplane stairs with Lenny, my white glove over his tan hand. I had olive skin, too.

"I'll go," I raised my hand.

"I thought I'd ask you anyway, Phyllis," said Miss Stuckey. "Since you're a concert pianist."

Miss Stuckey had called me a concert pianist ever since she heard me play "Malagueña" with the jazz band drummer, Charley Steele, at the high school talent show. I'd pounded out massive chords of Spanish passion on the school's Steinway to make students sit up and pay attention, but I knew I was a slight fraud. "Malagueña" was really a showboat piece, a fake classic. I was tired, however, of being earnest and unnoticed.

"Girls, remember," Miss Stuckey said as she half-sat on the drab gray, school issue table next to the record player and stack of Rhythmette records. "The Clark County Sheriff's Mounted Posse and Mayor Gragson will be there, but you are the real representatives of Las Vegas. Most out-of-state people have no idea there are *real people* here. Show those New Yorkers that we're not just specks of dust or whistle-stop creatures little better than the lizards. Do us proud!"

On Sunday evening, I polished my boots, dusted off my black hat, and dressed in my Rhythmette outfit—a one-piece coral jumpsuit with fringe dangling from the yoke and the bottom of the short shorts. I checked myself in the mirror. My long black hair curled under in the official Rhythmette page-boy; my lips were outlined with the patient strokes of a lipstick liner; my eyelashes stood straight up after I'd curled them with my eyelash curler. I powdered my already oily nose, though I'd just washed my face. Anxiety, maybe.

Karen honked the horn of her large-finned Chevrolet at six forty-five, and we drove to Sill's Drive-Inn for a cherry lime rickey. I fished for the maraschino cherry until my fingers were numb from the ice. It evaded me, clinging to the very bottom of the glass.

"I wish we didn't have to do this," Karen said. "I've got tons of homework."

"I do too," I said, "but this is the New York Philharmonic. Who could pass up the opportunity?"

"What do you know about them that you didn't know before five days ago?" She made a loud sucking noise with her straw.

"Everybody's heard of the New York Philharmonic."

"Sure, Phyllis. What do you know about them besides their name?"

I dug deeper into my crushed ice, almost grasping the cherry, but not quite, having to eat more ice before I could.

"That they're an orchestra from New York. What's wrong with that?"

"You're acting different, that's all."

"Maybe I am different. Maybe I'm more like the people in this philharmonic than I am like a Rhythmette. Maybe I want to *be* music. Maybe I want to go somewhere besides Sill's Drive-Inn. You know?"

"Hurry up and finish. We're almost late."

We picked up three other Rhythmettes, Nancy, Cheryl, and Valerie, Cheryl wearing too much perfume, and drove out to McCarran Airport—a long, low, sleepy adobe building. The parking lot was full for a Sunday night as the five of us marched in step and tossed a few high kicks to the muscular clouds wallpapering the sky. We said "hi" to the two skycaps who saluted us back.

"You girls with the Rhythmettes?" one of them asked, the gold on his front tooth reflecting spokes of light as he talked. "I see you in the paper time to time."

"Yes," Karen answered, but then we heard a plane descending on the airport runway. "We've got business with that plane right there."

The five of us ran through the almost empty lobby and through the French doors to find the other Rhythmettes and watch the plane taxi in. We shouldered through the crowd, saying "Excuse me," and stood behind a man in dark blue shirt and pants holding his arms high in the air, narrowing them to parallel as the plane closed in. Then a crew of two wheeled a stair ramp tight against the cabin.

All day, I'd thought about how I'd posture myself next to the conductor. Casual? Dramatic? My leg almost touching his on the stairs? Me waving to the crowd as if I'd just flown in myself. But there wasn't much of a crowd.

We watched the silver door swing open against the side of the silver plane which was silhouetted against the melodramatic sky. Great mounding clouds glowed an end-of-the-day rose as the stewardess appeared in her red lipstick, pillbox hat, tailored suit, and white gloves. She motioned the mayor, who held the key to the city, the president of the Las Vegas Symphony Society, and the ten Rhythmettes up the stairs. As we climbed, I strained for a glimpse of the conductor's black hair streaked with premature gray and his sharkskin gray suit with the black knit tie.

Then he appeared. He was framed by the arch of the airplane door. The Embodiment of Music. My heart riddled my chest as he lifted both arms above his head and made two Vs with his fingers. I watched his beautiful teeth emerge in a smile for the photographers. I looked at his deep olive skin, the powerful lines in his face, the intensity of his expression. And for a moment, I stood in a faraway field of green and yellow—me at one end, Lenny at the other—and both of us lifted our arms and ran through anemones and dandelions until we stood toe to toe gazing into each other's eyes. I imagined him stroking my hand and saying it was an artist's hand, and that he wanted me to play "Malagueña" with the New York Philharmonic. He'd talk to the percussion section right away. We'd have castanets, maracas, the tapping tips of the snare drummer's sticks for accompaniment. And then I returned to the warm Las Vegas evening, feeling more alone than before, looking up at The Lion as the hot wind swirled the tips of my hair.

He descended the first three stairs in an aureole of light—the setting sun burnishing him with magnificence, even holiness. I held my breath as he brushed past me, but he seemed distracted, other things on his mind. Maybe music filled every fold in his brain so he couldn't see me standing there.

One step below me he accepted the key to Las Vegas; one step below me he paused for photographers. The mayor, the Symphony Society's president, Karen, Nancy, Valerie, and Cheryl were with me on the stairs, but I felt alone, as if I were the only one who counted for this man. I knew Bach, Scarlatti, symphony etiquette. But more than that, I understood the artist—the world behind the eyes, the elegance of nuance. The conductor and I had more in common than he could know.

But he looked through me and the other Rhythmettes as if we were a surrealist painting—the lights of Las Vegas flashing against the fish-scale sky behind our black cowgirl hats, distant neon traveling its circuitry, a hot wind blowing across our cheeks, the air overheated from a 110-degree day. We were mere strokes in a painting, no one in particular to him.

Lenny, Lenny, don't you see me, Lenny? I know music. I know sforzandos and crescendos. I've had three piano teachers.

He descended a few more stairs, past the other Rhythmettes, and flung one arm high for the photographers. The Rhythmettes were now a receding frame, a background for Lenny. Photographers shouted and flashbulbs popped. He was now five steps below me, waving to the Jaycees and the Sheriff's Posse, stretching his silver suit jacket away from his hips. My eyes were riveted on his form, and I kept hoping he'd walk back to me and let his hand fall to my shoulder, that he'd look at me and say, "Talk to me."

When the photographers turned to go, Lenny could have changed directions and put one black shoe on the stairs. He could have reached out and said, "There you are," if only he'd been sympathetic to the high velocity vibrations quivering behind him. But he only looked straight ahead.

Suddenly, he seemed an enlarged photograph, a powdery man, a substitute for the real thing which was still back in New York composing music. I felt as if I could reach out my hand and put it through him, as if he were the projected movie halfway between the screen and the projectionist's booth.

He tossed his graying hair, walked through the gate in the cyclone fence, and left us in his wake.

The next morning, the *Las Vegas Sun* ran a picture of me standing behind the conductor on the ramp next to the airplane in my black cowgirl hat. I was smiling. But I was the only newspaper reader who knew about the smile because only the bottom half of my face showed in the picture. My eyes were lost to the top edge of the photo. Lenny looked distracted, uncomfortable, a little nonplussed by the Wild West welcome.

The following day, the day after the concert, I heard that Lenny said he'd never come back to Nevada: It was impossible to perform for such an audience; conditions were too difficult. But nowhere in any of the newspaper interviews did he mention that the Las Vegas Rhythmettes had welcomed him or that the Young Friends of the Symphony had sat above him so appropriately, their young bodies molded from the desert sand and wind, sitting stiffly in black dresses, black suits, and white gloves to pay respect.

The breath of culture, given so briefly, was taken away suddenly. Maybe I should have crowded closer so I could breathe him in, his New Yorkness, his power to make music with a flick of his wrist, his hands that unlocked doors to Carnegie Hall. Maybe I should have been bold and touched his sleeve, stolen some of his charisma, his knowledge, his culture. But I let it walk right by me, unable to reach out and touch it or keep some of it for myself. I let him get away.

Or maybe I should have said, "Lenny, you've walked past something wonderful!" But I'd faded into the background like desert sand. I should have gone back to McCarran when the orchestra was waiting in the lobby, surrounded by their cases of violins, cellos, violas, and double basses.

I could have talked to him and said, "I know we're like the wind that blows past your eyes, you shrinking into your suit to ward off its impact. I know the beauty of the desert is hard to see, a place where nothing but scrub brush grows."

But Lenny, you didn't have to leave in a huff. Didn't you notice the Young Friends of the Symphony? We tried, Lenny. And I was prepared. I learned complicated rhythms and studied scales.

You couldn't see, Lenny. I am music; the desert is music, too. You decided too soon. Your judgment was swift, and maybe, just maybe, it was wrong. Lenny, Lenny, why didn't you notice?

THE ROSE

*J*t was hard being a rose. Especially the kind of rose Sister Bradshaw, our special guest for Rose Night, was telling us we should be.

"Be like a rose, young ladies," she said to the semicircle of attentive fourteen year olds, each dressed in the most formal dress she possessed—Mary Lynn in stiff coral net; Kay in pink satin; I in two horsehair slips, a velveteen skirt, and a white lace blouse lined with acetate rayon to preserve my modesty. "And that includes the thorns."

The Mutual Improvement Association for Mormon teenagers, was held every Tuesday night at the Fifth and Sixth Ward house. It had a steeple tapering to a modernistic pinpoint, acres of soft green carpet inside, matching green cushions on the chapel's hardwood benches and on the folding chairs in the classrooms. It was the scene of instruction in eternal values, the ground school for celestial marriage, the setting for Rose Night.

Our regular MIA Maid teacher, Sister Wadsworth, had prepared us for Rose Night for months. "It will be the most special night of all six years of MIA," she told us often. "One of the most precious experiences of your young life. We'll have Sister

Bradshaw, a former runner-up for Nevada Mother of the Year, and a photographer from the *Las Vegas Review Journal* for this important occasion."

Sister Bradshaw was known for her inner beauty and womanly virtue. My mother said we were lucky to have her as a speaker. She gave her speech in a pink linen suit, a massively ruffled-at-the-throat pink nylon blouse, and closely curled hair. "All roses have thorns," she was saying.

I remember the word "thorns" sounding harsh as it came out of her cotton candy mouth, and I felt uncomfortable in my stiff horsehair underslips and acetate lining. I wouldn't have minded being a rose who smelled beautiful and mesmerized people with her fragrant petals and her deep velvet textures, but a rose with her thorns intact? I didn't have any thorns I knew of and wasn't interested in cultivating any. Life was tough enough.

"And now for the grand finale." Sister Bradshaw smiled and glowed and seemed excited as fifteen MIA Maids of the Las Vegas Fifth Ward—Leslie, Connie, Mary Lynn, Kay, Beth, Gaylee, Marilyn, me among them—sat anxiously in a semicircle on soft green cushions awaiting the big moment of the Rose Night lesson, the ritual we'd heard about from older girls who weren't supposed to tell.

Sister Bradshaw began by lifting a single white rose from the throat of a slim crystal vase. It trembled in her hand as she held it against her chest. It seemed like a prayer. "This is a pure white rose," she said, carrying it to Mary Lynn who sat on the end of the semicircle. "Touch it. Stroke it. Handle this in any way you'd like. I want you to become familiar with every part of this rose." And then the long-stemmed rose was in Mary Lynn's hand, trembling even more as she tried to hold it in a place where the stem was smooth.

"Take note of the thorns on the stem," Sister Bradshaw said to all of us. "Notice how hard it is to hold this flower without being pricked. Thorns make people handle a rose with care." She was glowing even more pinkly. "Remember that."

Mary Lynn rubbed the edge of the petal between her thumb and forefinger, then slid her finger deep inside the rose where the petals joined together. "It's like velvet," she said, then passed it to Kay, Kay to Beth, Beth to Leslie, until each of us in the row had taken the rose into our hands, stroked the white petals, rubbed them between our fingers per instructions, inhaled the flower's perfume.

When Lola, who sat on the other end of the semicircle, handed the rose back to the former runner-up for Nevada Mother of the Year, Sister Bradshaw held it high as if it were the Statue of Liberty's torch.

"Now girls, do you think any decent young man would want a rose that's been handled, passed around to everyone, felt by hands that have been who knows where?"

We all shook our heads no, the fifteen witnesses of the bruised rose. Its limp head was hanging, its white petals wounded into a squalid shade of brown.

She looked at us rather sternly. "No one, I repeat no one, wants a used rose. Your husband will want a girl who's fresh as the morning dew, sparkling, alive, brand new. Don't let the boys handle your body. Don't let them touch you in private places. Those places are yours to save for the man who'll be your husband. This fine man will take you to the Temple to recite holy vows before God for all eternity. He'll smile tenderly at you as you kneel across from each other at the altar of the Lord. He'll reverence you above all women because you've saved yourself just for him and your eternal marriage, the kind that lasts forever."

She paused and took one last sweeping glance of the girls before her. "As a memento of this precious night, I'm giving each and every one of you a long-stemmed rose to take home with you to press into your Treasures of Truth book. And," she began to whisper, as if these words were the most precious of all, "I bear witness to the truthfulness of these things, and I pray God will help you through the trial before you."

Sister Bradshaw bent down by the refreshment table and pulled a long white cardboard florist's box from under the floor-length tablecloth—an intricate Belgian linen cloth that was Sister Wadsworth's best, she'd told us. Then she opened the lid, unstapled the plastic wrapper with her fingernail, and handed a rose to each girl. As she did, she hugged each of us against her pink cheek.

When she stopped in front of me and handed me my rose, her eyes bored straight into mine. "I know you'll remember this unsullied rose and this night always. God be with you."

I wanted to cry over the beauty of her intentions. She was a nice woman, I could tell. But I needed to think, fast. When I sat back down on my green-cushioned folding chair, I started. And I kept at it while Mary Lynn gave the closing prayer and blessed the refreshments standing ready on Sister Wadsworth's Belgian tablecloth.

There was my cousin, Lee, who took me into his parents' chicken house when I was nine. He told me to take off my underpants while the chickens pecked at the hard earth close to the toes of my shoes. Luckily, he didn't know what he was doing. He loosened his pants to his knees, lifted his miniature penis in his young hand, and touched the side of my buttocks. When it brushed against my skin and I felt goose flesh rising on my arms and legs, I told him I didn't think we should be doing these things. I'd once been scolded for playing doctor with my friend Marie. At age five, we'd been exploring our mutual anatomies on the top of her bunk bed when Marie's mother opened the door and caught us with our legs spread wide apart, me with a magnifying glass in hand. She didn't accept our story about wanting to be doctors when we grew up.

And then there was my neighbor, Leonard, who was a junior in high school, a new boy on the block who'd just moved to Las Vegas from Mississippi. He came over one day when I was twelve and home alone. I told him I liked books. He asked to go up to my bedroom to see which books I liked best. I told him to follow me.

As we sat on the bed, opening the cover of a Nancy Drew mystery, he suddenly pushed me down on the chenille bedspread. There he was, on top of me, holding my wrists together and pulling them above my head, his large hand able to hold both wrists in one fold of his fingers.

"I don't like this," I told him, still uneducated about the possibilities. I didn't like his weight on me, the rub of his Levi's on my sunburned legs, and the way his lips were leaving a wide trail of saliva as they wandered over my cheekbones and eye sockets and temples, and I felt as though a snail was crawling over me, its body suctioned to my face.

"You'll like this," he said, pushing his hips against mine. I felt an unwelcome clump of muscle pressing against my tender pubic bones, almost bruising them. "You and me, Phyllis."

He was like a crab, the way his arms and legs wrapped around me, and I couldn't breathe. I couldn't find a way to get air into my lungs. "You're too heavy," I said.

"Only for a little while. Relax."

"Get off me!" I picked up the Nancy Drew mystery and, when Leonard didn't move, hit him on the side of the head. "Get off." Then I pushed against him with all my strength and rolled out from under him, the feel of his rough Levi's still alive on the skin of my legs where my shorts ended, the feel of his tight lips that didn't kiss but scavenged my face, his crab-like body wrapped around me, entangled with my arms and legs and trunk and body and mind.

"Don't ever do that again," I said, pointing toward the stairs. "I want to be your friend, but don't ever do that again. Understand?"

Leonard never came back. He didn't want to be friends. But it didn't matter. He wasn't what I would ask for if I had three wishes.

By the end of Mary Lynn's closing prayer, I could honestly say I was a pristine rose. I'd kept all invaders away. Of course, not many had tried to bruise my petals, at least nobody I was interested in. But I was still an undefiled rose, an untouched one just beginning to blossom from a tightly wrapped bud of pale yellow. I decided I was a yellow rose, like sunshine, like Texas, like the two or three triumphant daffodils that bloomed in our straggly garden every February. White was too bleached, too pale. Pink was too much like Sister Bradshaw whom I didn't quite trust because of the way she said "thorns." Red was too strong: red blood on fingers pricked by thorns, red punch that stained the tablecloth, red sunrises that warned sailors, red lipstick smeared on Sister Wadsworth's eyetooth, red inflamed pimples on my face. I'd be a yellow rose. Perfect.

Perfect even though on Saturdays I spent time at Ronnie Freed's house. She wasn't a Mormon; she'd just moved to Las Vegas from Brooklyn; and she never talked about being a rose. She knew makeup: powder, blush, eyeliner, waterproof mascara, the right shade of lipstick for a particular shade of skin. Joyous Red by Max Factor was her favorite color, and she applied it with a lipstick brush, outlining her lips with minute strokes, then filling them in with the tube.

Touching the unfortunate curve of her nose, she divulged a deep-hearted secret I was never supposed to tell anyone else. "A nose job. In two more years," she said. "When I'm sixteen." But when we compared boobs, as she called them, she was way ahead of me, a 36-D, with a sumptuous, womanly figure. "All the boys would die for this." She squeezed her breasts with both hands. Then she gave me a crash course in bending over and letting what little breasts I possessed fill my 32-A brassiere. This way, I could maximize the cleavage. She also gave me a written test torn out of some magazine to determine my chances as a great lover: Had I ever had someone's tongue in my mouth? Had I let a boy put his hand on my breast? Below my waist? How often did I dream about sex?

I started tagging along with Ronnie and a few other girls on weekends. We went to parties I never told my parents about. There were beers I didn't drink and cigarettes I didn't smoke. But I was fascinated with the comings and goings of the boys who disappeared into bedrooms with some of the girls. There were sounds on the other side of the door: laughing, the give of bedsprings, "Oh, baby, baby."

I found myself wishing someone nicer than Leonard would invite me into the bedroom, even though I wouldn't have known what to do. I'd only given fast, runaway kisses on the elementary school playground. I spent the evening with my back against a strange living room wall, observing, sometimes thinking about being a sweet-smelling desirable rose, sometimes viewing myself as a rose rising out of this garden of weeds. That's how Sister Bradshaw would have put it had she seen me standing there so chaste, so prim, so proper. She wouldn't have known I was utterly afraid no one would ask me to do anything.

"The values of the world are not the values the girls should seek," Sister Bradshaw was saying to Sister Wadsworth as she helped her serve the refreshments—7-Up punch tinted pink, cooled by an ice ring with frozen roses suspended inside; cupcakes decorated with white frosting roses. "They don't know the people of the world accept less when it comes to high values. Let's hope and pray the girls can save themselves for their one and only."

If Sister Bradshaw had asked me when she handed me a napkin with a rose embossed in the corner, I would have said there was no doubt I was saving myself for that golden warrior from the sky. I was prepared. I was saving all my gifts just for him. But then why was I standing against the wall of Fred Soskin's house, watching people do the dirty bop, listening to Elvis sing "Heartbreak Hotel" and then Fats sing about finding his thrill? Why was I acting as if I were a perfect rose when I was really dying for someone to touch me, to feel my velvet skin? It was one thing to be an unsullied rose because I wanted to be. But what if nobody stopped by the garden to admire me? That would be worse than sullied.

When I thought about it further, I had to face facts. Nobody at this party seemed interested in my kind of rose—long-stemmed, gangly, too big of leaves, too tight of bud. I was awkward.

But even at MIA, even in the church house, even as I listened to Sister Bradshaw and agreed with every word—yes, of course, I wanted to be fresh for the man who would someday ask me to be his wife—I knew I wanted someone to want to touch me. And I didn't want him to be an ephemeral man, a spirit like the Holy Ghost, me like the Virgin Mary. I wanted to feel his skin. I wanted someone to bend me backwards, inhale me, and kiss me for a long, long time.

Sometimes, instead of hearing the still, small voice whispering to me about right and wrong, I wanted a real hand to appear, connected to a real body with flesh and sinews, a hand that knew how to stroke me in just the right way, lips that would know how to kiss me without leaving a trail of saliva on my face.

A rose is a rose. It is a beautiful aromatic flower attracting people with its scent. Some want to bury their noses in the flower, sniffing, trying to possess the fragrance, hold it inside until it is part of their being. But a rose grows out of the earth smelling like roots and bark and damp earth and twigs. And a rose can bud and blossom and open wide until it loses its petals without anyone ever putting a finger to it. So why did I have to be a rose? Why couldn't I just be a girl? Girls didn't have petals, stamens, pistils, or thorns either. Not in real life.

Bobby Jack didn't appear until I was seventeen. The first day I saw him I liked the way he looked. Smooth. Street smart. Cool. He wore plaid shirts I liked, had an air of worldliness that made me trust him. He wasn't trying to be perfect. And I knew he was the one who could touch me the way I wanted to be touched. Something about his dark brown eyes. They were easy to get lost in. They weren't afraid, and they knew me. He instinctively knew I was a rose wanting to be held.

Bobby Jack frightened my mother and father because they sensed I wasn't afraid of his touch. He had the power to bend me and make me lose myself. He had the power to make me forget the spiritual realm where no one made physical contact, where everything happened inside the mind, and the power of God surged in the heart and breast and head but never touched the flesh.

"You can't go out with him," my mother said. "He's no good. He has no values. He drinks and smokes, and you want to be with him? What's happened to you?"

" 'No man is good save God,' " I quoted scripture.

"Don't try to dazzle me with your fancy footwork, young lady."

Every night when I was supposed to be somewhere else, we ended up at Bobby Jack's apartment. His mother was always gone. She was a cocktail waitress on the night shift. We watched television, we sometimes did homework or made peanut butter sandwiches, but our fingers and hands would always find each other, and we'd end up in his mother's bedroom on her blue-flowered bedspread. I just wanted him to touch me, to connect with my skin, to hold me as I'd never been held before. And he did touch me.

He touched my neck, my face, my legs, my arms, and sometimes, just briefly, my breasts. I breathed heavily and pulled him on top of me until I could feel the buttons of his plaid shirt hard against my chest. And I touched him—the backs of his ears, the brisk ends of his haircut, the slimness of his waist. He rocked and twisted with me and played the game I'd been wanting to play for so long.

Shadows of perfume bottles on his mother's dressing table grew tall and narrow against a wall of the moonlit room. The short nightgown hanging on the back of his mother's door began an incandescent life—gathers of colorless nylon alive and swaying to the rhythm of our two bodies. The world was stretching out of the shape I knew it to be.

The idea of The Rose had been sealed tightly into the folds of my brain, however, and I felt as though, while Bobby Jack and I touched each other on that one particular night, a red rose was rooting in my heart and growing out of the neck of my blouse, complete with thorns.

"I'll hate you if you ever make me do anything against God's will," I heard myself saying as we stared at each others' eyes in the dark, Bobby Jack propped on his elbows.

"You mean sex?" he said, running his fingers through one side of his hair.

"Yes, but don't stop touching me. Not ever."

"We could get married," he said.

For the first time, Bobby Jack felt heavier than my body could support. I pushed him away, to the side, on his back into the blue garden of flat, large-petaled flowers. Marriage meant the Mormon Temple for time and all eternity, a worthy man kneeling across the altar, white pearls, white lace, white roses. Marriage to Bobby Jack meant a wheezing minister in a dusty Nevada town. The Garden of Love Chapel. He'd leer at us while his fat lips muttered sacred words of matrimony.

"No," I said. "I've got to save myself."

"What's wrong with me?" He doubled a pillow to raise his head.

"It's not that," I said as I sat up on the edge of his bed and straightened my hair and blouse. "It's something that won't leave my head. I've got to save myself."

"You're the one who encourages me, almost like a nympho-maniac. Save yourself for what?"

"I want more," I said as I found my pink flats askew on the blue carpet and scrunched my feet back inside. The shoes felt cold, stiff, had no give for the warm feet trying to find a way to leave inside them.

"You're all screwed up." He rolled off the bed and threw the pillow at me, its case covered with blue flowers. "Get out of my life."

"I can't," and I fell back into the floral bedspread and started to cry.

He crawled across the bed, knelt beside me, smoothed my hair. "It's okay, Phyllis. Isn't it enough we love each other?"

I shook my head no as I sat up again. He'd never heard Sister Bradshaw's talk on Rose Night. How could he understand a girl with a body who really didn't have a body?

Here was Bobby Jack stroking my hair and touching me and telling me I was not only real, but something he wanted and something he desired. I wanted to hand him the rose that seemed to be growing out of my blouse, its roots in my heart, and say, "This is yours," but I couldn't.

In my mind, I broke the stem of my rose at its base and held it up high. It became a torch, flaming with the fire of God and the fire of what could be if I followed the true path without faltering, the stony path, not the broad and easy road. I mustn't take the easy road. I must follow the way filled with brambles and thorns. It could lead me to God, where someday I could touch him and know he is real. To touch God must be greater than anything I could ever imagine.

Then Bobby Jack wrapped me in his arms one last time and rocked me as if I were his child. The torch disappeared. All I could hear was the ticking of his mother's alarm clock as he rocked me to its rhythm.

I looked up into his eyes in the dark. They reflected the moonlight fanning through the high windows, and they seemed to know more than could be said—the calm of an afternoon being swallowed by the sinking sun, the sound of a note when the voice has stopped singing. I wondered why I could see so far into him in this darkness, into this person I suddenly knew I loved for more than the fact that he touched me.

I closed my own eyes and wondered if I could see into myself so far, if there was anything like that inside of me. At first, I saw only the blank wall of the dark lowered over my eyes. But then, slowly, gradually, behind my eyelids, I knew it was God holding me, God touching me. Yesterday, today, forever.

FREMONT STREET

*I*f you've ever been to Las Vegas, you've been to Fremont Street. You may not have noticed the street itself because of the thousands of persistently flashing lights that confuse night and day and make you think you've arrived at the palace of the end of the world. But it's there beneath the speedway light bulbs racing off and on and inviting you inside for a game of roulette, craps, or keno.

Fremont Street. I can't think of it as a street, actually. There's always the shine of light on its surface as if it were patent leather. Maybe it isn't a street, but a way into a world where you can't close your mouth, or into a cave where you find the wizard who'll teach you all you need to know about escaping.

When I was there, Fremont Street seduced me with the mystery of the shifting bodies on its surface—winos, losers, Nellis Air Force Base flyboys who sometimes whistled at me, big-time spenders looking for the next game. It seduced me with the sound of money, with the blaring clothes people wore, with the possibility of dying my hair champagne pink and gluing rhinestones to my forehead.

The street was a temptress, leading to wide doors where guards said, "No, you can't come in here." But the doors weren't doors, they were giant sucking machines inside of which money fell into slot machine trays, stacks of chips grew tall and short on green felt tables, and men with I-know-the-world-and-everything-about-it-and-you-can't-faze-me expressions were dressed in green aprons, their faces pointed like foxes.

Protected by the seagull-wing fins of a '59 Chevy, my friends Karen, Cheryl, and I dragged Fremont street on warm nights, the windows rolled down, all of us craning our necks to see something to gasp about. Carloads full of teenagers, tourists, and flyboys cruised the street to the Union Pacific station, turned around, cruised back. Up and down Fremont.

Sometimes flyboys would yell at us: "Hey, baby, what's happening?" Karen gunned her engine to say we weren't interested. We wanted something else from Fremont Street—a genie to puff out of a light bulb, casino doors to vacuum us inside before we could protest, the golden nugget on the neon sign to fall and make a crater on the hood of Karen's Chevy.

But the street, as animated as it seemed when we drove or walked on its surface, was only a street after all. It couldn't give anything to anyone. It could only lie in the sand and let pass what would. We were only another moving molecule on Fremont Street—into its brightness, out of its brightness.

When we drove onto the side streets and away from Fremont, we saw the backside of the casinos sagging under the weight of millions of light bulbs screwed into their sockets, the buildings with nothing but alleys and shadows behind them. And behind those shadows were even darker streets where the shapes of our everyday houses waited for us. Only the moon, the dim street-lights, and Karen's headlights illuminated the pathway to our own front doors.

The lower end of Fremont Street wasn't far from the high school, one block away. At lunchtime, when the air was throbbing with cheap sunlight, Cheryl, Karen, and I descended the stairs of the pink-stuccoed high school and tripped down the sidewalks in our C.H. Baker pointed shoes (pink, baby blue, orange, avocado, purple, and chartreuse for $8.99 a pair—whatever matched our outfits). We passed the girls and boys gathered into an elite knot on the front lawn, making our usual comments about the girls in their cashmere sweaters beaded with tubular glass, their wool tartan skirts with jewels embedded in brown squares. No one seemed to notice our departure. We crossed Bridger Street and walked past apartments with drawn shades where night people waited for blood to return to their heads.

Once a month, we saved our money for lunch at the El Cortez, a hotel on Fremont Street. It was a second cousin to the casinos nearer the depot, but we felt big time as we ordered open-faced turkey sandwiches from a waitress in a thigh-length wench costume, two-thirds of her breasts rising like yeast below her lifeless face.

I crunched my kosher dill and laughed with Cheryl and Karen about how, when we got rich, we'd rent a helicopter and Elvis and land on the front lawn of the high school and see who was elite then. We'd buy angora sweaters and a Cadillac convertible and maybe a miniature poodle with a diamond collar for the back seat. We'd buy matching felt skirts with pink poodles prancing across the hemline.

Even as we talked, I could hear the handles of slot machines in the other room being pulled and pulled and pulled. I wondered where the money came from, even considered the possibility of the machines incubating their own coins and giving birth to the money, money, money while lights flashed and bells rang.

For some reason, though, I knew this money could never be mine, even if I had a truckload of coins to spend and pulled the same machine's handle all night long. It would be devoured again and again, the nickels and dimes and quarters food for the hungry slot machines rather than extra cash for Phyllis.

It seemed to me, as I cut into the turkey on my open-faced sandwich with my water-stained knife, that somewhere, in some great sky, someone had chosen the lucky and the unlucky, the winners and the losers. Luck wasn't granted because someone needed or deserved it, or I'd be the luckiest one alive. I deserved a boyfriend, a nomination for Homecoming Queen, even a few curves in my body, after all. But I hadn't been chosen. Someone must have made some decisions even before Fremont Street was laid in a straight line on the desert, before bricks were stacked or boards were nailed into casinos.

As much as I wanted a helicopter with Elvis on board, a gold Cadillac, and a chance to prove myself to the students who ruled the front lawn of the high school, I knew the money in the other room would never be mine. It belonged to Fremont Street and to the lucky. I'd have to get what I wanted in some other way, maybe from God if I kept saying my prayers every night before bedtime.

In May, the town celebrated Helldorado Days. There were a kangaroo court, a full-fledged carnival, and major parades on Fremont Street. Local businesses sponsored floats; the veterans marched in ranks; the schools sent their drum majors, majorettes, and marching bands with glockenspiels to compete for first place; and the horsey people blanketed their mounts in thousands of pounds of silver tack and waved to everyone, even as their horses plopped road apples on Fremont. When Budweiser Beer Clydesdales pranced in front of us, their heavy, white-feathered legs clopping on the street, we clapped and cheered from the sidelines, but mostly because someone or something would soon step into their huge mounds of fresh-steaming, green manure.

Because of Helldorado, I had a chance for Fremont Street to

give something back to me—a chance to be noticed by the clique on the front lawn as well as the people of the town, a chance to ride high above the pavement in the light of full day, not over-shadowed by the blinking lights and the sound of money. I'd already marched with the Las Vegas High School Rhythmettes in last year's Oldtimers' Parade and kicked my share of road apples to the side. But that wasn't enough. I'd never quite felt noticed.

Miss Stuckey received telephone calls almost daily with requests for a Rhythmette to appear on television, have a picture taken with the mayor, model for a local fashion show, serve as hostess for a Rotary wives' tea. Everyone in the community seemed anxious to show support for the youth of Nevada.

"I received a call this morning," she said as I exited the shower in the girls' locker room. I was dripping water on the miniscule tiles. "It was from the executive secretary of one of the casinos on Fremont Street. The owner wants to have one of the senior Rhyth-mettes be the queen of his hotel's float for the Beauty Parade. They're going to use real flowers, even for the queen's costume. Would you be interested?"

I almost dropped my towel when I realized how big the door was that was opening before me. A queen. No one had ever asked or nominated or elected me for such a thing. *Queen*, I said to myself as I continued to drip on the tiny tiles. *Queen Phyllis*.

I'd watched "Queen for a Day" on television; I'd seen young women crowned for Miss this and that; I'd read about chorus girls being past queens of cities and counties. I liked the idea of Queen Phyllis, even for one float for one day of the year.

"I'd like that," I told Miss Stuckey.

"All right," she said. "The secretary said to be at the casino for a fitting this afternoon. Go over there after school, and take the stairs next to the roulette wheel. If a security guard stops you, tell him you're on your way to the administrative offices. It's at the top of the stairs. And the parade is two weeks from Sunday."

Sunday, I suddenly realized, panic tightening my lungs. I pulled the towel more tightly around myself. *The parade was on Sunday. My parents! The day of rest. The Lord's day.* My stomach clenched. My forehead perspired. Here was good versus evil again, set on a table before me, waiting to be examined: a good Mormon girl's joy comes from obedience to commandments versus Phyllis Nelson's chance to be queen.

As I walked down the narrow passage between the hardwood bench lined with smelly sneakers and other girls dressing in front of their marine green lockers, I felt the old feeling of being bumped to the outside of life. So often I'd stood apart while I longed to wander from the tight circle of the righteous just once. This time it was only to ride on the top of a float in the bosom of flowers and crepe paper and tinsel. A queen on the float gliding above the crowd cheering for the late, but lovely, bloomer as she passed. The queen.

But never on Sunday.

I turned to see if I could catch Miss Stuckey's attention and tell her I'd forgotten something important I had to do on that Sunday, but she'd gone back to her tiny office covered with newspaper clippings of the Rhythmettes marching at the Pikes Peak Rodeo and the Pendleton Round-up, smiling their thousand-tooth smiles for the cameras, their page-boy hairstyles glistening with highlights. "My babies," she called the Rhythmettes. She herded us like fine sheep, watched whom we dated, checked our grades every term, told us to stand up straight, told us to be proud of ourselves as not everyone was able to make the marks required to be a Las Vegas High School Rhythmette. She'd turned her sweatshirted back to me and was busy examining a schedule on her clipboard. What could I say to her anyway? I'd already said yes.

Why did it always have to come to this? I wondered as I towelled the last water from my calves and the arches of my feet. I only wanted to ride on a float in the open air and sunshine and wave to the people, to be dressed in flowers which were one of God's most beautiful creations, to make my mark on Fremont Street. I wouldn't be fornicating or lying. I wouldn't be taking the Lord's name in vain. But I wouldn't be honoring my father and mother, either. They wanted me to keep the Sabbath day holy and follow the commandments given to Moses, then to the Israelites, then to us. I needed to obey if I wanted to find my way back to God.

Please, God, I prayed as I pulled my brassiere off the hook in my locker. *Please, God. Understand about this.* I hooked my bra together, then climbed into my underpants labeled Wednesday. *You're the King. I only want to be queen for a few minutes. Have a heart. You wouldn't mind just this once, would you?*

I could hear water dripping in the shower stall and the echo of the solitary drops, one by one, hitting the tile, splashing the floor, the sharp sound of water working its way through the tile, wearing it down in the course of time. Time was so long. If I was only one drop of water to God in one split second of time, what would it matter if I rode on a float down Fremont Street? One small ride didn't have anything to do with God.

The casino was one of the biggest. I recognized the owner's picture, bigger than life, in the lobby, a shiny black and white of him with his arm around his son, Ted, who went to the high school and was already an alcoholic, though a desirable one—lots of black, curly hair, a king of hearts smile. I hoped I wouldn't run into Ted because he might tell his father he'd chosen the wrong girl to ride on his float, a girl outside the knot that owned the front lawn of the high school. He'd say his father should have done more checking rather than trust Miss Stuckey. Luckily, he was nowhere in sight. Neither was his father. The secretary smiled, her eyes peeking out of cat-eye rhinestone rims.

"You must be Phyllis Nelson," she said, pursing her lips and tipping her head slightly as if to say, "How cute you little high school girls are, and isn't this casino wonderful to care about our city's homegrown?" She tugged at the string connecting her glasses to her neck.

"Come this way, and I'll take you to Mrs. Rubinstein. She'll fit you for the costume." When she rolled her chair back and stood up next to me, she looked surprised. "My, you're one of the tall ones, aren't you?"

"I'm on the tall end of the line, yes."

"And you're rather thin, too," she glanced back at me nervously as she opened the office door. "Well, follow me. Mrs. Rubinstein knows how to fix anything."

She walked down a long hall with marbled carpet—browns, golds, oranges, rusts, swirling in the hallway. She swayed when she walked, her buttocks sharply accenting each step, her high heels sinking into the cushioned carpet and leaning to the insides. She stopped to rub her finger on one of the hall light fixtures. "Dusty," she said. We walked and walked, up stairs and down stairs, each step feeling heavier to me. What was I doing here? Why was I following this woman down long halls? Where was she leading me? And each step became burdened with the argument again.

"You only want temporal pleasures," one side of me said.

"You want to keep me from having any fun," the other said back.

"It's such a puny thing," side one said, "to be a queen on a float. That that should be more important to you than keeping God's commandments says more about you than I'd like to hear."

"Why shouldn't I be a queen? Who am I hurting? Absolutely nobody."

"Except yourself," said side one.

"Give me a break!"

"This way," the secretary said as she opened a door marked wardrobe. "Mrs. Rubinstein will take care of you." She patted my arm as I passed through the door, then held onto the inside and outside doorknobs, leaned back, and scrutinized me one last time. "Mrs. Rubinstein, this is Phyllis Nelson for the Beauty Parade float. You'll know just what to do, I'm sure. She's one of the Rhythmettes, you know—the ones you see in the newspapers all the time. Have fun in the flowers, honey." She closed the door.

I turned to look at Mrs. Rubinstein, who was a marked contrast from the rest of the hotel. She was small, her hair pulled severely to the nape of her neck and secured in a bun. She wore pince-nez and looked at me over the tops of them. Her lips were colored a slight coral, but she wore nothing more on her face. She looked both very young and very old in her transparent long-sleeved blouse of white nylon. Underneath the fabric, two obvious straps dug into her shoulders, pulled tight by heavy breasts and a slightly round stomach. As Mrs. Rubinstein hunched over gathered fabric and leaned close into her work, she reminded me of a leaf turning colors under the autumn sun, slightly brown at the edges, yet still a vibrant gold in the center. Something about the gold made me say what I said, the words out of my mouth before I even thought them.

"I love God," I said before she had a chance to say anything.

Without looking up, she gathered her eyebrows together, then opened her basket of thread, needles, thimbles, and tapes. "Good for you, dear." She narrowed her eyes even further, raised her head, and looked intensely through rather than at me, no words. Then, remembering our business, she picked up a small green notepad.

"What is your waist size?" she asked. "Hips? Bust? Hat size?" She wrote on the green pad and measured the questions I couldn't answer. And while she slid the tape around my hips and breasts, I promised myself I'd pray the whole time I'd be riding on the float. I'd think about God and his sunshine and his people all the time I rolled down Fremont Street. I'd light my candle for him, and my smile would be filled with his grace. When people looked up at me, they'd see God's essence, not Phyllis Nelson dressed as a float queen. If I wasn't actually on the float, it would be okay if I was there.

"We'll beef up your chest," she said. "God didn't give you much in the way of breasts, did he?" She reached into a drawer and pulled out two sizes of foam pads. She put one size over one of my breasts, then the other, and as she did, I noticed the pale blue numbers slipping out from under the lace at her wrist.

"We'll use the thickest one," she said, and made notes to herself on the pad. "And I want you to come in at twelve o'clock on the day of the parade. Our makeup artist can give you some glamour, bring out the beauty in your face, fix your hair to show off your features. You shouldn't let it hang in your eyes, dear. We'll make you into a first-class beauty. False eyelashes, pluck the eyebrows, plump up the chest. You'll be a beautiful queen in a raiment of flowers. Do you like the idea of being dressed in flowers? Novel, isn't it?"

I wanted to talk to Mrs. Rubinstein. I wanted to forget about the flowers and ask about the numbers. I wanted her to tell me about those people—how they put the numbers there and if they hurt her, or if they pushed her if she stepped out of line, or if they ever stopped to notice she was God's child.

"Were you my age?" I pointed to the numbers on her wrist.

She looked directly into my eyes, and I saw large slivers of time—fierce, sad, dank—and I knew she'd never worried about riding on a float down Fremont Street or whether she was a queen or not, except when the nights were long and she shivered under a thin blanket and called out to God, who didn't hear her. Maybe she wondered if there was any love at all, not the least bit con-cerned with the kind of love that would ask to be honored as a queen.

"So you love God, do you?" she said.

"Yes, I do," but then I suddenly saw the power of God staring out of her eyes, a bigger God than I'd ever seen before: a God so magnificent he was all the flowers in the world at the same time, a God so frightening he was all the withered flowers in the world. And then she sat down and lifted her needle, its thread, the amorphous blue metallic fabric onto her lap. She leaned back over her work as if I'd already left the room. I started to say something, but there were no words left between us.

As I walked over the swirling carpet, I knew I didn't have to ride down Fremont in a car, on a float, or even in a taxi. I'd telephone Karen. I'd ask her to take my place. She'd be overjoyed to be the queen, just as I had been.

Fremont Street. I walked along its sidewalks in the late afternoon on my way to the bus stop. Shadows from the casinos across the street touched the curb next to my feet. They were long shadows of buildings housing treasures that were part of my wishes by day and my dreams at night.

But I'd been behind these buildings; I knew they were made of regular things like bricks, glass, stone, and clay, even though they were camouflaged by the lights and their storehouses of games, diversions, machines that seemed to manufacture money, tables where the lucky became rich, rich, rich when their hands curled around a stack of chips.

But as I walked along the concrete sidewalk lining Fremont Street, I imagined tables surrounded by men with slicked-back hair, standing at the tables forever until they were covered with cobwebs and their pointed fox faces stiffened with frost. Yet they still rolled the dice to decide who would be lucky or unlucky, who would win or who would lose, even though they suspected the decision was made before dice were invented.

If you've ever been to Las Vegas, you've been to Fremont Street. You've seen the flashing lights that hide the simple lines of the asphalt street, the fact that the street begins and then ends, the fact that no one ever stays there. You know it's only a street to walk on until you reach the doors that open in, then open out again. You know it's a black ribbon of asphalt rolled out on the desert floor until it passes through a bouquet of brilliant flowering lights which attract the honeybees and you and me. You sniff its scent, want to hold it in your nostrils like cigarette smoke.

But you know you're walking into a daylily in reverse, still open at night, inviting you to sniff its perfume. And you know when a flower never closes, it isn't a flower. It's only Fremont Street.

AN AUGUST NIGHT

*T*his is like other nights I've known, except it's different. Outside my bedroom window, lightning splits the night, and its roots branch into crooked tendrils. Inside, the heat hangs like soggy leaves over my bed, my face, my skin.

The sky is so alive with strobe light and heroic thunder that I'm almost fooled, as I have been on other August nights. But then I remember this is the way the desert night cries wolf. There won't be any rain. It's only the heat playing tricks with the sky and with me as I try to find sleep.

After a busy half hour, the thunder rumbles a last time and rolls eastward. The lightning does a final, halfhearted dance on the sky's stage. But the heat stays. It hasn't moved anywhere. It's as insistent at night as it is at high noon when the sun stretches across the sky and crowds everything else out of its way. It's the main show in town, bigger than the Strip, the neon lights, or even Elvis. Those things are paltry next to this heat and the big brazen sun that shows up every day with no mercy. Nothing is bigger than the sun and this twenty-four-hour heat.

As I lie here in my soggy bed, I toss the top sheet from side to side. My hair is wet, my back is wet, the folds at the backs of my knees are wet, the sheets are wet on my bed in my upstairs bedroom behind lace curtains.

I've had dreams of being something. I've even asked God's blessings on my life and the lives of my children to come. But when I lie here in the unforgiving heat, the swamp cooler unable to make a difference, I am small, and I want to tear my nightgown off and lie here with nothing on—an immeasurably immodest desire, especially if angels are watching.

I wish the lightning would split my walls open. I wish the thunder would rip the sky apart horizontally after the lightning ripped it open vertically. Then I could be sucked into that gaping black hole on a cool breeze. I want to feel something besides this heat even if I'm only one young girl in one small house on a street in the least populated state in the Union.

I'm going away to Brigham Young University in two weeks. I'm going to escape this life—away from Bobby Jack; away from the call of the chorus line; away from the people who are going nowhere, making nothing of their lives; away from the desert with its bad attitude about universal order—its helter-skelter city planning, trailers parked next to yucca and creosote bushes, its drifters. I'm going somewhere and leaving this chaos behind.

But I can't think about that right now. My hair is soaked with perspiration. I can't find a cool spot on my pillow or on my bed. Every inch of the sheet and the pillowcase is hot, stifling hot. I want to be resurrected, rise out of my deadweight body and these cotton sheets.

So I do something I've never done before. Slowly, looking up to see if God might be watching, I roll up the bottom of my nightgown. I feel my midriff bare, then my breasts, my collarbone, my chin, the nightgown over my head, flung to the floor. I look again, hoping no angels or my dead brother will see me, and I pull one leg out of my underpants, then the other. I lie there, spread-eagled. No one is watching. No one is witnessing this rebirth. No one sees this moment when I'm stark naked before God and all the eyes of angels.

At first, I cross my arms over my body to protect myself, then I roll back and forth across the sheets to cause a breeze. There's no escape from this heat. There's no escape from this body. There's no cool place. Even if a hand touched my skin, it would be too hot, too clammy, too heavy. I want a breeze. I want a cold pillow where I can rest my cheek. Something cool.

I creep downstairs to the refrigerator, dragging my robe behind in case my father or mother hears rustling in the night. I examine my long tan legs in the light of the refrigerator's open door—the front of me illuminated, the back of me in shadow—and utter a quick prayer: May my parents sleep soundly and not find me standing thus in the light of the refrigerator. Quickly, I crack three ice cubes out of the tray and surreptitiously carry them back upstairs with me and my robe.

Lying back in the stifling sheets, I set the ice cubes to sail across my stomach and over my arms, across my cheeks. It is so hot. But I'll be out of here soon. I'll be at Brigham Young University where I can escape this place, this phony city, this Las Vegas of the mind—desert, heat, gambling, no sense of higher values. No one at BYU will know about me here in the dark, feeling the ice turn to water on my skin, molten trails of wetness across my body, the shine accentuated by the moonlight now filling my window. I'll be out of here soon. Safe in the high mountains.

As I stretch until my toes curl over the end of the mattress, I think about yesterday afternoon, sitting at a white lacquered baby grand at the Frontier Hotel. I'd adjusted the white leather stool, turning the knobs on both sides to lower it and make room for my legs. Then I'd settled the piano lid on the long lid prop. I didn't have to worry about overpowering any soloists yesterday. I was in the main room where the Frontier stages its floor shows. I couldn't play too loudly.

"Here's your check," the woman in a white linen sailor suit and a gold chain necklace said. She waved a thin yellow draft across the yawning cavity of the open piano. "Just keep some kind of music going so we won't have dead spots. When the contestants do their free posing, give them about ninety seconds. Nothing draggy. I've got a lot to do, so accept my thanks now. Okay?"

"Fine," I said, folding the check and stuffing it in my wallet as she disappeared.

I'd brought a few pieces of sheet music I thought might be appropriate—"Stouthearted Men," "The Marine Hymn," "The Sunny Side of the Street"—anything I could think of for the competitors soon to be revealed to the sparse, slowly gathering audience with Mai Tais and margaritas in hand.

As I spread the scores on the music desk, the spotlight brightened. An announcer appeared in a royal blue brocaded tuxedo with black satin lapels. His hair was puffed wide and tall over a good-morning sunshine tan, and a microphone cord trailed him down the runway.

"Good afternoon, ladies and gentlemen. Welcome to the first annual Mr. Nevada Contest." He paused, and I supposed he wanted some loud chords on the piano, some kind of bass-note drum roll or fanfare. I played a few tentative chords, then waited for my next cue.

"We have ten contestants today, some from our local body-building club on Charleston Boulevard, the rest from Reno's Pump House. These young gentlemen have spent countless hours battling the iron and subsisting on vitamin pills and protein powders. They deserve our utmost admiration. Yesiree, folks! Sweating like they do, lifting barbells day after day, bench pressing, squatting with tonnage on the bar. And," the announcer almost whispered, "one of these young men, on this very day," then he gradually increased the power of his voice, "will be chosen to represent Nevada at the nationals in Los Angeles for the Mr. Olympia Contest."

He paused again, and I started playing a very legato version of "Stouthearted Men"—something to blend in and not be too obvious.

"First, our contestants will be evaluated for symmetry and skin texture. Then we'll introduce each one individually for free posing. Bring on the show!"

I launched into "Stouthearted Men" full steam, but felt funny about it after a few bars. It didn't seem to set the right tone for these ten bronzed bodies walking single file down the runway, their arms unable to touch their thighs, their muscles gleaming with oil. I couldn't quite figure suitable music for this contest and wished I were Jerry Lee Lewis.

The contestants stood shoulder to shoulder until the judge told them to turn a quarter, then another, and another, until they'd turned all the way around. But what I saw when the contestants turned in my direction was someone I'd seen before. Someone familiar from the halls of Las Vegas High School, someone who'd been a ninety-pound weakling, a lizard kind of guy who smoked behind the auto shop building and made himself invisible the whole time he attended LVHS. I stared at this particular body-builder who resembled a dim recollection—Ronald Wooge.

After the contestants disappeared en masse behind the curtains, the emcee called each of them out again, one by one. When I heard "Ronald Wooge of Las Vegas" and he paraded past me to the tune of "Sunny Side of the Street," I gaped at the sight. His waist was tapered like the tip of a triangle; his muscles stood out from his body like soloists. I'd never seen Ronald without his shirt, but the physique before my eyes didn't match the one I thought I knew. As he struck a double bicep lat spread pose, I realized this was a Ronald I never could have imagined. This was Ronald large in the world, Ronald reconstructed.

Silently, I laughed at the thought of Ronald Wooge in the Mr. Nevada competition. How could he bring himself to this arena when he was only Ronald Wooge? But Ronald standing there, posing so seriously, inspired something in me. I was sorry I'd laughed. I wondered what I could do for him in the next ninety seconds? What kind of music would help the judges single out Ronald Wooge and make the teardrops on his thighs glint more brilliantly? Maybe "Whole Lot of Shakin' Goin' On," just like Jerry Lee, those walking bass octaves and key-bending glissandos to get the audience toe tapping, rocking in the aisles, to get the judges thinking this was some amazing thing—this Ronald Wooge transformed.

But I was riveted to the safety of the printed notes in front of my face, the staves of "Sunny Side of the Street." I was afraid to venture into something wild and uncontrolled for Ronald, the kind of crazy music I sometimes played in the privacy of my own home. Ronald tried to pose with confidence; he tried to spread his muscles into the largest span ever known to man. But something kept both of us in check, some element of history no one else could see, except maybe Ronald and me in our own private thoughts.

Maybe I failed Ronald, maybe he failed himself. Despite all those hours coaxing those muscles out of obscurity, he only came in third in the Mr. Nevada Contest. Despite my efforts to play a no-holds-barred, ninety seconds of music for him, I only jazzed up "Sunny Side of the Street" a little bit. Maybe "failed" is the wrong word. Both of us were still shedding our old skins yesterday afternoon. And Ronald did come in third. I'd have to call that some kind of triumph.

He keeps walking down the runway of my mind as I try to make peace with this August night and this heat. I can't find anything resembling sleep. I can't find anything to comfort me. This heat presses like a giant's palm pressing down and down and down until I don't exist—only heat exists. My ice cubes have melted already; my sheets are bunched into a topographical map; I'm bare in the moonlight, and still, there's no relief.

This oppressive heat keeps me from the mirage of night dreams where there's a breeze blowing through palm fronds and I'm beautiful and cool in the shade—detached, serene, beyond all this. This is the self I'm taking to BYU, to my new life, but tonight it seems I'll never get to my dreams. I'm turning over and over in these damp bedclothes. I'm filled with an insatiable longing here with nothing on in the dark, the moon lighting the curves of my thighs and accentuating the shadows.

I think of a few hours ago, me walking through the Showboat casino, wrapped in a fox stole that was hot, hotter than now, and a silver-spangled bikini underneath.

The casino was busy, as usual—people mesmerized with the prospects of money falling out of machines into their hands, numbers on the roulette wheel spinning and a wooden ball settling, wheels turning, croupiers watching. It's not as though the whole casino stopped dead still when my best friend Karen and I appeared in our furs. I'd begged my parents for modeling lessons to give me the grace I needed to survive, and now Karen and I were modeling for Betty's House of Furs to make money for our freshman year at BYU. We'd been through the casino several times already in yellow coordinated sportswear, tennis dresses, and jeweled evening gowns. Now we were presenting our grand finale.

While dealers slapped cards onto green felt and overhead mirrors reflected flashing diamond rings and earrings and rhinestone tiaras, we heard Betty, the owner of the House of Furs, announcing Karen's name from the place where she stood in the dining room.

"Break a leg," I said.

Karen took a deep breath. "Why did we let Betty talk us into this bikini business? We are so dumb."

"I agree," I said, wiping perspiration from my lip. "The only consolation is, no one will ever know about it."

"See you in a minute." Karen walked under the wrought-iron arch, her bare legs exposed beneath the hem of the mink coat, her black-patent high heels sliding across the carpet.

While Betty explained the detailing on Karen's coat, I waited outside, next to the cigarette machine, wrapped tightly in the long silver fox stole even though it was a ferocious August night outside. My forehead perspiring, even though the casino was chilly, I could see Karen through the grillwork separating the dining room from the casino.

When she stopped at a table close to me and executed a full circle turn, I suddenly marveled at the sight through the wrought-iron curlicues in the grill. Here was my normal, everyday friend, Karen, who usually wore tennis shoes and white Levi's. Here she was in powder, eyeliner, rouge, dark lipstick, and a lush mink jacket. Suddenly she was an exotic hybrid—lush, intriguing. I'd never seen her like this before. She was beautiful. But the people in the restaurant had no idea that a flower had opened right in front of them. They busied themselves with their green, red, and yellow melon balls and the excision of the pineapple's tough core from their tidbits.

When she reached the portable staircase Betty had brought along for the show, I watched Karen strike a pose we'd learned in modeling school—one hand on her hip, the other held out to the side, its fingers arranged as if she were about to drink a sophisticated cup of tea. Quickly, she opened the right side of her mink jacket, then the left to offer the briefest glimpse of the gold lamé bikini Betty was now describing. But then she blushed like the BYU coed she would soon be. She closed the mink coat too quickly, rushed past the tables, the feeble applause, past the cashier, up to me with her eyes rolled back and an aura of "let me out of here."

"Thank goodness that's over," she whispered. "What if Bishop Huntington saw us doing this?"

"You really look beautiful."

She laughed.

"You're going to knock 'em dead at BYU," I said. "Maybe we're finally blooming, you know, like everybody said we would."

"Betty's calling your name, Phyllis. You better get in there. See you back at the room."

I listened to Betty describing the stole wrapped triply around my torso. "Our little Rhythmette, Phyllis Nelson, is wearing an unusual fur stole, pieced in the tongue-and-groove style common to fine furniture-making but rarely seen in furs."

Was I blooming like Karen? Was I changing as I'd always been promised in my heart-to-heart talks with my mother? And just who was this underneath this fur, and why was she wearing a bikini?

"Notice the exquisite tailoring," Betty was saying. "Consider the reputation of the furrier."

My three-inch green suede heels carried me into that restaurant; my fingers were buried in fox fur as I walked across the diamonds-within-diamonds carpet, past people's tables while they ate their bacon, lettuce, and tomato sandwiches and sipped their Cokes. My thighs were firm at the bottom of the stole; the base of the curve of my buttocks was exactly level with the laminated table tops.

I wasn't Thora and Herman Nelson's daughter. She wouldn't be doing this. I must not be a very good Mormon because I was wearing a bikini under this fur coat and was about to show it to everyone. I wasn't anybody I'd ever known.

Stopping at a table where three men had weathered faces and pale white foreheads, I said "Good evening" and posed like a statue—one knee bent, the other leg out in front at a slant, one hand on my hip, the other hand holding the tip of the stole to show the fox's head. They were more interested in what they'd have for dinner, it seemed. I smiled until my smile began to tremble at the corners, but I waited until the men, who looked as if they knew something about ranching, looked up. I did my full turn. "Two thousand for the stole," I told them. "Betty's House of Furs on Oakey Boulevard." I handed them Betty's business card.

"No thanks, ma'am," one said. "I've shot a few of them critters in my time when they messed with my wife's chickens. Just hung 'em over the fence to dry." The men chuckled and returned their attention to the dinner section on their menus.

"Enjoy your evening," I said with a cotton mouth, knowing I'd been of no use to Betty or her House of Furs.

I finally arrived at the staircase where I was supposed to reveal myself and my silver bikini to these passive people chewing on white bread and tomatoes. I climbed to the top of the three-stair case, smiling somebody else's smile. I took a deep breath and slowly unwrapped the fox. Air, sweet precious manufactured air, vacuumed the sweat from my face and arms and rejuvenated my clammy skin as the fur peeled away. Goose flesh prickled my arms and stomach.

"Notice the European cut of the bottom of this swimsuit," Betty said as I let the fox stole slip to the floor except for the end I held in my hand. "High on the hip. And notice the unusual overlapping of the sequins. A sumptuous rendition of a bikini, wouldn't you say? Brought to you by one of Las Vegas's own Rhythmettes. Isn't she a doll, ladies and gentlemen? Let's hear it for this lovely little model."

To the scant applause from one or two people, I turned on the staircase—a slow, languid turn as if I were a windup doll revolving on a music box pedestal. Slowly, slowly—the legs, the arms, one side, the back, the other side, the front, as people ate and talked and sometimes glanced. But no one was attuned to the fact that something important was happening, that a soul was swimming in unknown waters.

I tossed the fur over my right shoulder but didn't wrap myself

back into the cocoon as I should have. One half of the bikini exposed, I walked with long-legged strides past Betty and her microphone, past the ranchers, out of the restaurant, into the casino
where the mirrors were gleaming even brighter with reflected
streaks of hair oil, glossy lipstick, and shot glasses.

When no people looked up from their games, I walked up to
a twenty-one table where a young dealer had three nondescript
patrons. He shuffled the cards as if they were water and as if water
were his game. I stood absolutely still until he lifted his eyes my
way for one quick second. His eyes returned to the game, but I
stood even more still until he looked up again. This time, the deck
of cards in hand, he raised his chin slightly and kissed the air as
if it were me. He nodded his head in a slow yes.

That was enough. I smiled my own smile and turned for the
lobby and the automatic doors that opened to the heat of the night
and the smell of water sprinkling the grass. I crossed the parking
lot to the room where we changed clothes, but paused between a
pale green Imperial and a red Mercury with lightning chrome on
its sides to slip the fox off my shoulder. I could feel the heat from
the cars, even though the sun was down. I could feel the heat from
the asphalt. It clung to my skin as I stood there listening to cars
idle and crickets chirp. It felt as though I wore it—a hot velvet
dress wrapping my shoulders and waist and legs, a velvet drape
hanging in thick folds around my ankles.

Now I feel as though there's nothing in the world besides this
bed and this August night. I can't escape it, no matter what I do.
It's under my skin. No matter where I go, no matter who tries to
teach me what, the heat will always be with me. It will penetrate
my dreams when I'm in the high mountains. It will spread thickly
across my night landscape like a plague.

Sometimes it will come carrying a stark round moon; sometimes it will bring lightning and the rumble of thunder inside

stone-colored clouds. It will always find me and remind me of broken rocks, mesquite, sand, the sun, and snakes crawling out of old skins wearing new ones. It will hover over whatever I'll become.